SOCCER

Skills and Tactics

ENES
18

SOCCER

Skills and Tactics

Tim Edward

Foreword by Harry Redknapp

This is a Parragon Book
This edition published in 2004

Parragon
Queen Street House
4 Queen Street
Bath, BA1 1HE, UK

Produced by Atlantic Publishing

Origination by Croxsons PrePress

A catalogue record
for this book is available from
the British Library.

ISBN 1-40543-951-3

CONTENTS

FOREWORD

HARRY REDKNAPP

When Bobby Robson was asked what on earth he was doing still involved in the cauldron of top-level football in his late sixties, the answer he gave would have struck a chord with football fans everywhere. The Newcastle United boss said it was his work, his hobby, his life; and anyway, who wants to go shopping on a Saturday afternoon when there's a game on? Point taken.

Football unites us all. Whether you're a David Beckham, a minor league amateur or someone who just likes a kickabout in the park, the game remains the same: beautiful to behold and really quite simple.

The two big differences between the top players and the rest of us mere mortals are fitness and skill levels. We can all train hard, become faster and stronger. But what about skill? You've either got it or you haven't, right? Wrong!

Consider two of the greatest players of the modern era, George Best and Kevin Keegan. Best had amazing natural ability - that's true enough - but he still practised day after day on the streets of Belfast where he grew up. He would spend hours kicking a ball against gutters, garage doors, even doorknobs, learning how to control the awkward rebounds. And later he used this skill to brilliant effect on the biggest stages, cheekily playing one-twos off the shins of bewildered defenders!

Kevin Keegan's rise to the top is an even more dramatic example of the need for dedication and practice. He had nowhere near Best's natural ability and was told as a youngster that he would never make it. Keegan was utterly single-minded, however. He worked incredibly hard, making the most of what talent he had. Liverpool plucked him from lowly Scunthorpe, and he went on to captain England and become European Footballer of the Year. There's hope for us all!

So the message is clear: whether you're blessed with a lot of natural talent or not, you need to work hard on your game. And when you've perfected a skill, keep working on it until it becomes second nature. Why else do you think David Beckham stays behind after training to pepper the goal with his free-kick thunderbolts?

This book might not turn you into a Beckham, but it covers all the skills you'll need to become a good player, no matter what your position. There are top technique tips to improve your individual performance. There's also a detailed analysis of positional play, formations and tactics. This is an increasingly important part of football, for no matter how good you are on the ball, you have to remember that it is an 11-man game. Well-organized sides who attack and defend as a unit can often come out on top against a group of more talented individuals.

Whatever level you play at, or whether you're just a keen watcher, this book will help to improve your knowledge and understanding of the Beautiful Game.

McDonald's
Carlsberg

SKILLS

PREPARATION

Steven Gerrard goes through his warm-up routine.

Preparing for a game used to mean little more than a bit of passing and shooting practice while the captain tossed up in the centre circle. The influence of continental coaches such as Arsene Wenger and Gerard Houllier has helped to change our thinking about the way we prepare for a match or training session.

It starts long before you get anywhere near the pitch. A good balanced diet is important. Football takes a lot out of you, and you have to replenish what is lost. Plenty of fresh fruit and vegetables, lean white meat, fish and pasta will give your body the proteins, carbohydrates and vitamins it needs. Burgers, pizzas and chips are okay now and again, but don't live on them! Your body will also lose fluid, so drink plenty of water.

Warming-up

Before any strenuous activity, be it a training session or full-scale match, you should warm up thoroughly. Football is an explosive game. You might be standing still one second and going flat out the next. If your muscles aren't well stretched and loosened, you run the risk of straining them. A thorough warm-up is especially important if the temperature is low. Cold muscles need time to reach their optimum working level. If you cut corners here, you could end up on the injury list instead of the pitch.

Stretching the quadriceps

To stretch the quadriceps adopt the positon shown, making sure you are well balanced. Repeat three times with each leg, holding the position for twenty seconds. Never 'bounce' or over stretch.

Players from the the Italian squad. Always warm-up thoroughly before a training session or full-scale match. Start with a gentle jog, gradually increasing your stride.

The upper body

Patrick Vieira going through his well-rehearsed warm-up routine. Although leg muscles get most of the attention, warming and stretching the upper body muscles is also important. These muscles include the stomach, back, side, neck and shoulders.

Stretching

Start with a gentle jog, gradually increasing your stride. Then do some side skips, using your arms to make a star shape. Now step it up to a side run, crossing the trailing leg in front of and behind the leading leg alternately. Work your way up to a flat-out sprint.

When you are warm, go through a stretching routine for all the major muscle groups. Obviously, the leg muscles will get most of the attention - that is, the hamstrings, calves, thighs and groin. Stretching the upper body muscles is essential for goalkeepers, but it is also a good idea for outfield players too. These muscles include the stomach, back, side, neck and shoulders.

The quadriceps

Frank Lampard (l) and Jamie Carragher supporting each other as they stand on one leg to stretch their quadriceps.

Steven Gerrard stretches his hamstring muscle from a kneeling position. The hamstring is the muscle at the back of the thigh.

Suppleness

For all stretching exercises, the movements should be gradual. Stretch into position and hold for twenty seconds, then release. Going through such a routine will increase the range of movement in your limbs. Greater suppleness will be an advantage on the field, and also help to prevent injury.

Warming down

Top athletes also go through a warm-down session after vigorous exercise. This is a shortened version of the warm-up, and will increase muscle flexibility over time. It also helps to prevent any stiffness that might occur.

Hamstring stretch

Sit on the floor and with your leg straight and then gradually move your outstretched hands towards your lower leg. Hold the position for twenty seconds.

STRIKING THE BALL

David Beckham practises his shooting skills

The ball can be struck using a range of different techniques and a variety of contact surfaces. You don't have to be a master of all of them - many top professionals aren't - but the more technical weapons you have in your armoury, the more complete a player you will become.

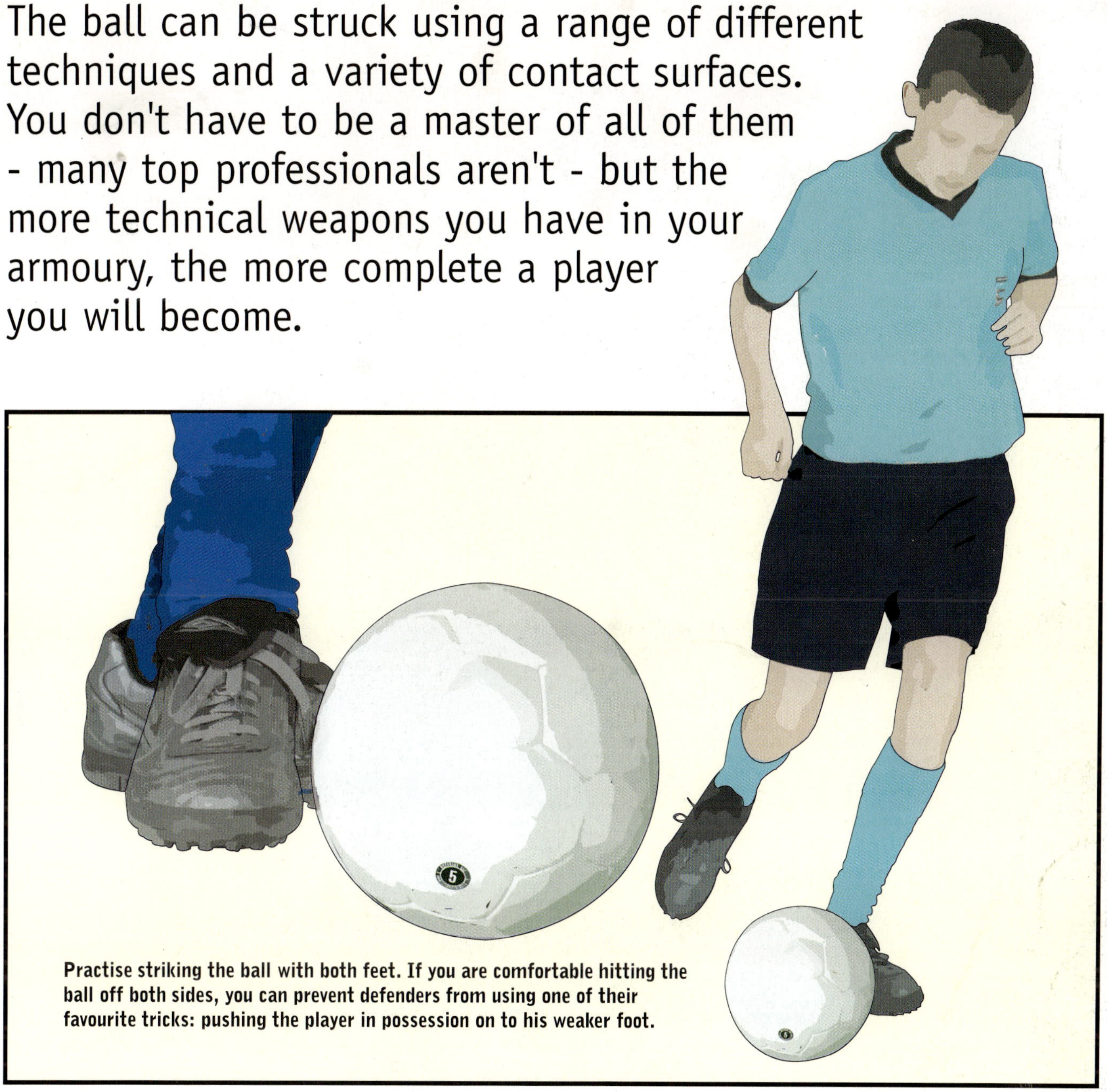

Practise striking the ball with both feet. If you are comfortable hitting the ball off both sides, you can prevent defenders from using one of their favourite tricks: pushing the player in possession on to his weaker foot.

Use both feet

One of the most common weaknesses is being one-footed. Many players use one leg to propel the ball and the other simply to stand on! Being two-footed has distinct advantages. First, if an opponent knows you will only deliver the ball with a particular foot, then you are removing one of the major uncertainty factors. Now, that may not always matter. There have been many internationals who have been almost exclusively one-footed. Knowing which foot a player is going to use to strike the ball and doing something about it are two completely different things. Nevertheless, if you are comfortable hitting the ball with either foot, you are preventing defenders from using one of their favourite tricks: pushing the player in possession on to his weaker foot.

The second advantage of being two-footed is that it can buy time and space. If you receive the ball on your weaker side, you will inevitably lose valuable time in transferring it to your stronger foot - possibly enough time for a defender to get in a challenge.

Finally, it should be noted that most ball-striking techniques are used for both passing and shooting. Both involve delivering the ball with a target in mind: with passing, the target is a team-mate; with shooting, it is the back of the net.

THE PUSH PASS

The basic side-foot pass, or push pass, is the bread-and-butter method of delivering the ball for all teams. The ball is stroked along the ground using the large surface area of the side of the boot. It is the most accurate and reliable way of striking the ball, but the amount of power generated is limited, so it is only useful over short distances. The pass-and-move approach to the game is all about accurate short passing; in effect, it could be said that the tactics of the modern era are underpinned by the push pass. In spite of its name, the push pass is often used by goal poachers to stroke the ball into the net.

- The non-kicking foot should be placed alongside the ball
- Head and body should be over the ball at the point of contact
- Strike through the midline of the ball. The striking foot should be at right angles to the direction of the pass
- Always follow through

Joe Cole making a side-footed pass. The ball is struck with the large surface area of the side of the boot.

DRIVING THE BALL

Despite the importance of the short passing game, it does have the disadvantage of being a slower, more methodical build-up. The more direct approach afforded by the longer ball can take several defenders out of the game at a stroke. David Beckham and Steven Gerrard are two of the best exponents of the long, raking pass. The side-foot technique is no use for hitting 50-yard passes; instead, the ball is driven with the instep.

There are two variations on the drive, depending on whether you want to keep the ball low or loft it through the air. The former is better suited to shooting, the latter comes into its own in long passing.

- **For the low drive,** the approach should be at a slight angle. The non-kicking foot is placed close to the ball
- **With toes pointing down,** strike through the centre of the ball
- **For the lofted drive,** approach from a slightly wider angle. Place the non-kicking foot a little behind the ball. Strike through the centre of the ball, but this time below the horizontal midline
- **When driving the ball,** most young players make the mistake of trying to hit the leather off it. Timing and technique are far more important. David Beckham regularly hits 50-yard passes and makes it look quite effortless

James Beattie of Southampton uses the drive to shoot for goal.

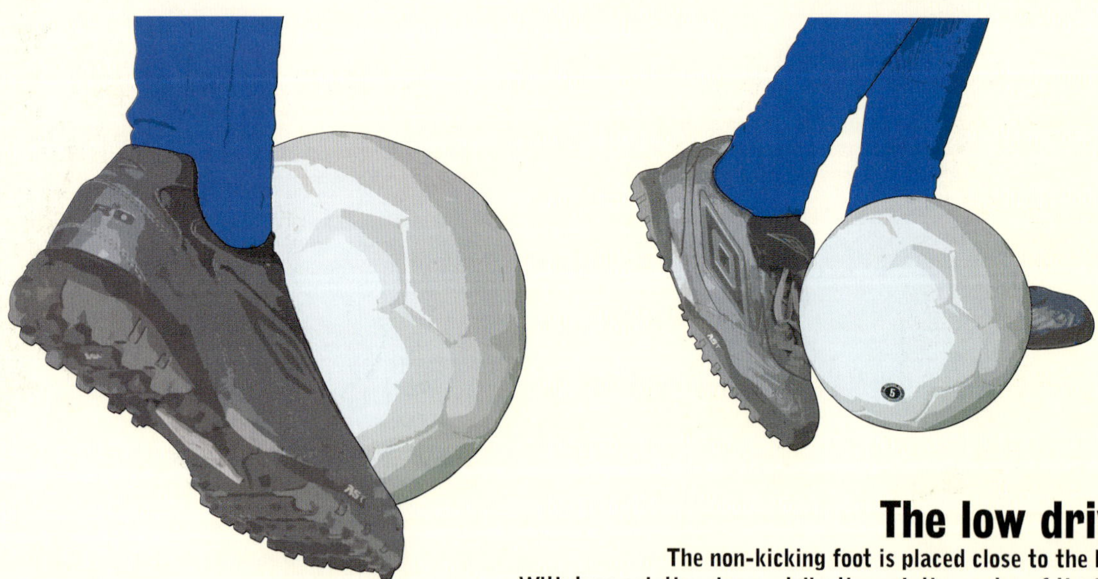

The low drive

The non-kicking foot is placed close to the ball. With toes pointing down, strike through the centre of the ball.

At one time, bending the ball was seen as a very innovative technique, the preserve of Brazilian maestros. These days, it is an extremely common skill. It is certainly not a party piece. Swerving passes can be used to take opponents out of the game, find team-mates who couldn't be reached with another kind of pass, and exploit space. Swerving shots can be used to bend the ball round a keeper's outstretched hand and into the net.

Sidespin

To swerve the ball you must strike it off-centre. Both the inside and outside of the foot can be used. In either case, sidespin will be put on the ball, which will make it travel in an arc. The balance between the power and spin on the ball, and whether it goes high or stays low, will depend on the exact point of contact. Striking the ball just off-centre will give more power and less spin; a more glancing contact will give more spin and less power. Similarly, striking the ball through the horizontal midline will keep the ball low; striking below the horizontal midline will make it rise. All these various permutations are easier to practise than to describe! If you experiment with striking the ball in all these different ways, you will soon begin to develop a feel for what kind of contact brings about a particular result.

SWERVING THE BALL

- **Practise swerving the ball** with the inside of the foot first
- **The kicking foot** strikes across the ball from inside to outside (ie from left to right if you are right-footed, and vice versa). Contact should be made around the base of the big toe
- **On making contact**, rotate the foot. This is often described as "wrapping the foot around the ball". It is the technique that David Beckham uses to such devastating effect in his long passing and from dead-ball situations
- **To swerve the ball** with the outside of the foot, place the non-kicking foot a little behind and to the side of the ball
- **The kicking foot** comes across the body from outside to inside (ie for a right-footed player the boot comes across the body to strike the left-hand side of ball, and vice versa). Toes should be pointing down at moment of contact
- **With all swerving passes** the follow-through is very important

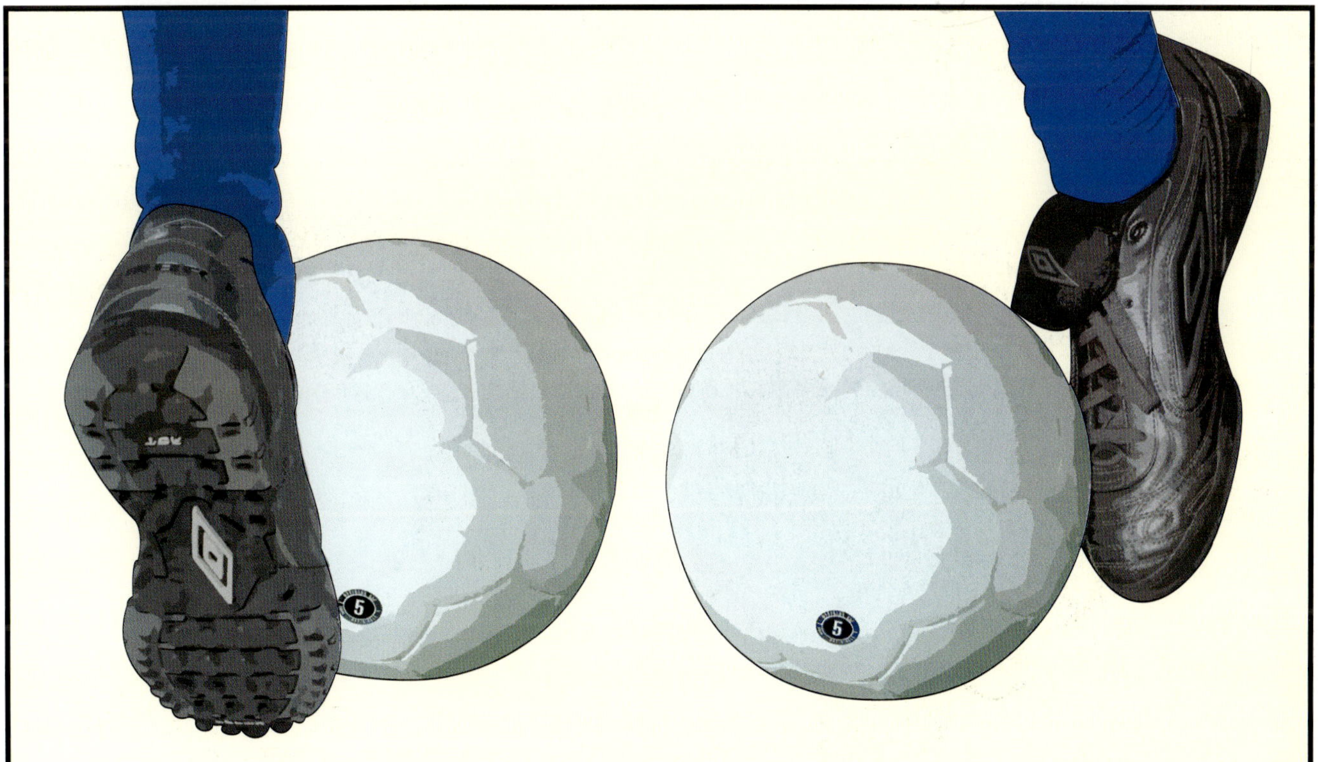

To swerve the ball you must strike it off-centre.

Rui Costa of AC Milan volleying the ball.
The big advantage with the volley - striking the ball first time instead of controlling it - is speed.

THE VOLLEY

The big advantage of the volley – striking the ball first time instead of controlling it – is speed. Defenders have little time to react, and if you are shooting, goalkeepers might be taken by surprise.

It isn't easy to strike a ball that might be coming towards you, going across you, or dropping out of the air. The key is to get your body into a good position early and not to abandon good technique in favour of a wild swing! It's timing that is required, not brute force.

Volleys can be defined in two ways: one is the part of the foot that is used to strike the ball, the other is where the ball is in relation to the body.

Side-foot or instep?

The side-foot and instep can both be used to volley the ball. The difference between the two is very similar to the difference between the push pass and the drive. In other words, the side-foot volley - just like the side-foot pass - offers greater accuracy and reliability but less power. An instep volley - just like an instep drive - generates a lot of power, but the contact surface is much smaller so there is a greater margin for error.

Generally speaking, the side-foot volley is used for an instant lay-off to a team-mate. If the ball is arriving at pace, the volleyer can cushion the ball as he guides it towards the receiver. The instep volley is often used by defenders clearing their lines or strikers shooting for goal.

Marc Wilmots of Belgium shoots for goal. There is more margin for error when volleying with the top of the foot rather than the side of the foot.

1. Volleying from the front

Either the side-foot or instep technique can be used from this position. If a power volley is required, strike the ball centrally with the toes pointing downwards. Make sure your body is over the ball. If you are leaning backwards, you won't be able to keep the ball down. That won't matter for a defender making a clearance, but for a striker going for goal it will almost inevitably mean the ball sailing over the bar.

The side-foot volley pass is really a midair version of the push pass. You must be well balanced on your standing leg. Guide the ball to the receiver with the foot at right angles to the direction of the pass.

2. Volleying from the side

This will nearly always be an instep volley. It is most commonly associated with shooting, though it can be used as a passing technique. The body rotates around the standing leg as you strike the ball. As the kicking foot comes across the body, there will be a natural tendency to fall away. This won't matter after you have gone through with the shot, but any loss of balance as you are shaping to shoot will almost certainly result in a poor delivery. Ideally, contact should be made through the centre of the ball. Sometimes, players err on the side of caution and get over the ball, driving it into the ground. Although this will take some pace off the shot, it is no bad technique to use since goalkeepers dislike balls bouncing in front of them.

Strike the ball centrally with the toes pointing downwards. Make sure your body is over the ball.

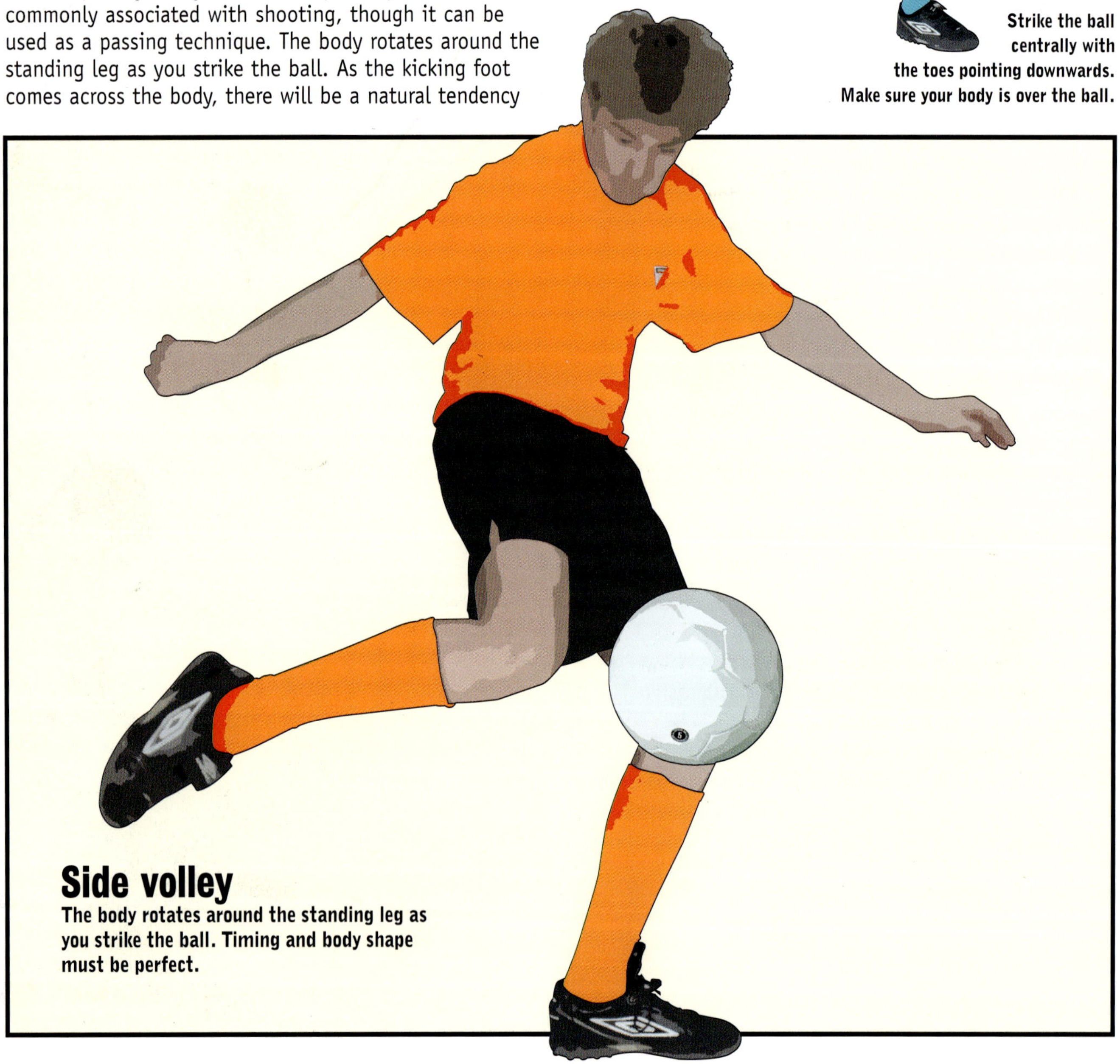

Side volley

The body rotates around the standing leg as you strike the ball. Timing and body shape must be perfect.

3. Overhead Kick

If you were grading the various football skills by their degree of difficulty, the overhead kick definitely would come into the "advanced" category. The margin of error with this acrobatic technique is extremely small. If your timing is even fractionally out, the ball can finish up well off target - and you may not make contact at all! Don't worry; even the pros can't manage a high success rate with this technique.

Confidence

Because the overhead kick requires perfect timing and touch, it really helps if a player is in good form and very confident. Having said all that, if the ball is in the air and you have your back to goal, the overhead kick can be just the thing to take an unwary goalkeeper by surprise. Of course, you could lay the ball off to a team-mate, or maybe control the ball and turn. Indeed, you will probably take one of those options most of the time. But occasionally, an overhead kick is well worth the risk. Like all snap shots, it has the advantage of cutting down the reaction time of both the defenders and the goalkeeper.

Strike with the instep

Take off with your kicking leg. Raise your non-kicking leg and lean back. Use your arms to maintain good balance, and keep your eye on the ball. Bring your kicking leg through and strike the ball with the instep. The leg should be outstretched, with toes curled forward so that you can get over the ball. This is particularly important if you are striking for goal, less so if you are in defence and merely trying to clear your lines. As the kicking leg whips through the ball, the non-striking leg naturally drops to act as a counterbalance. The way the two legs cross has given this technique its other common name, the "scissor kick".Be very careful when practising overhead kicks. Your non-kicking foot and hands should hit the ground first to break your fall. In particular, avoid letting your back, shoulders or neck take the full impact. The potential for injury is obviously greater on hard ground. For that reason, practise this skill on a soft surface, perhaps even using mats.

Thierry Henry makes an overhead kick. Take off with your kicking leg. The leg should be outstretched, with toes curled forward so that you can get over the ball.

Overhead kick

Your non-kicking foot and hands should hit the ground first to break your fall. In particular, avoid letting your back, shoulders or neck take the full impact.

THE CHIP

Hitting the ball up in the air isn't too difficult. Getting it up, over opponents and down again into a tight space (ball into the net!) is a little more tricky. This is when the chip comes into its own.

To chip the ball the non-kicking foot should be close to the ball. The kicking foot stabs down under the ball but does not follow through. The ball rises steeply; it is possible to get it over the head of opponents standing just a few yards away. The stabbing action puts backspin on the ball, making it hold up sharply as it pitches on the turf. This makes it a very effective weapon against a defence which is pushing up. If you can drop the ball beyond the last defender, and a team-mate can time his run to beat the offside trap, a goalscoring opportunity could be created. The chip is equally important as a means of beating an advancing goalkeeper in a one-on-one situation.

The Chip

The non-kicking foot should be close to the ball. The kicking foot stabs down under the ball but does not follow through.

Zoltan Sebescen stabs under the ball for the perfect chip.

The stabbing action puts backspin on the ball, making it hold up sharply as it pitches on the turf.

Japanese defender Alessandro Santos. From a well-balanced position a player can disguise his intentions.

HEEL AND TOE

The unexpected pass

Playing the ball accurately with either end of the foot isn't easy, and these techniques should be used sparingly. However, there are certain situations when using the heel or toe might be very useful indeed.

Use of the toe is really confined to 50-50 situations, when you're stretching to reach a ball before a defender or goalkeeper. In such cases, you may not have time to use a more orthodox technique. Stretching out to toe-end the ball past your opponent could mean keeping possession, or even a goal.

The use of the heel is a more deliberate ploy. A striker in the 6-yard box with his back to goal might attempt to backheel the ball into the net, and goals have certainly been scored in this way. More commonly, the backheel is used to give an unexpected pass. Because it reverses the anticipated direction of the pass, a backheel can catch opponents out. Since disguise is one of the non-technical aspects of good passing, the backheel scores highly in this regard. Unfortunately, if team-mates aren't on the same wavelength, a backheel can fool them too! This technique shouldn't be overdone; if it is repeated too often the element of surprise will be diminished. It is also best employed in the attacking third, as a wrong-footing pass to create a scoring chance. In the defensive third or midfield area, the risks would outweigh the rewards.

PASSING

Sylvain Distin of Manchester City.

Football is a team game. It is all about blending diverse talents into a tight, effective unit. A team that operates well collectively will perform at a much higher level than the skills of the individual players might suggest. To play as a unit, teams must be adept at passing the ball.

Accurate passing is the key skill in football. It is the means by which individual team members combine for a common purpose. A good pass employs three fundamental skills; selection, timing and execution.

Passing and movement

Virtuoso individual performances can win games, but they can't be used as the basis for a team's tactics, or a guide to a team's form. The first and foremost consideration of any top coach analysing a game is the quality of the passing and movement.

We have already looked at the techniques used for passing the ball. But passing is a skill, not just a technique. It isn't enough simply to learn how to strike the ball well. Let's look at some of the wider aspects of good passing.

Pass selection

The player in possession ought to have a range of passing options open to him. Good support play will ensure this is so. The player on the ball must then decide which team-mate to pass to. Every decision will have a risk/reward factor. A long through-ball, especially on the ground, is very risky but might be worth it if a goalscoring opportunity can be created. On the other hand, a 10-yard sideways or backwards pass might be risk-free, but neither does it pose any threat to the opposition. That isn't to say that the "negative" pass is always wrong. Indeed, moving the ball around in this way while looking for a good attacking opening might be the very thing to do.

To make pass selection as easy as possible, players must learn to play with their heads up. Your awareness of what is happening around you will be severely restricted if you spend too much time looking at the ball.

If weighing up the value of each pass isn't difficult enough, the picture can change totally in a second. This leads to the next consideration: timing.

SUCCESSFUL PASSING

Blackburn Rover's Barry Ferguson is completely focused as he delivers the pass. Gauging the weight to deliver a pass is crucial to its effectiveness.

1. Timing

Football is a fast and furious game. An excellent choice of pass one moment could be a poor option if made a fraction too soon or too late. The receiver has to share some responsibility in this regard. Well-timed passing requires both passer and receiver to be on the same wavelength. They may use little signals as a means of agreeing when and where the pass will be delivered. The more team-mates play together and get to know each other's game, the more automatic this process becomes.

Play with your head up

To make pass selection as easy as possible, players must learn to play with their heads up. Your awareness of what is happening around you will be severely restricted if you spend too much time looking at the ball.

2. Direction, height and pace

The decision to pass to a particular team-mate prompts several more decisions that have to be made. Are you going to play the ball in the air or along the deck? Will you play the ball to his feet or into space? How much pace will you put on the ball? Let's examine each in turn.

When judging what height of pass to make, remember that the ground pass is direct and will get to the receiver more quickly. It will also be easier for him to control. The downside to such passes is the risk of interception, particularly when played over distance. Aerial balls don't carry that risk, but their arcing trajectory gives defenders more time to react.

As a general rule, in tighter situations you should play the ball to feet. In a congested midfield area, for example, there won't be much space and a ball played even a couple of yards wide of the receiver could result in loss of possession. Down the flanks and behind the defenders it could be a very different picture. If a player has space in front of him to move into, then the ball could be played several yards ahead of the receiver without risk. Indeed, ball-to-feet in such a position could be a handicap as the move would suffer a loss of momentum.

3. Weighting the pass

Once you have got the height and direction right, you now have to get the correct weight on the ball. Too much pace will make it hard to control when played to feet. An overhit ball played into space is likely to run harmlessly out of play or to an opponent. Conversely, not enough pace on the ball, either when played to feet or into space, is inviting an interception.

4. Disguise

Finally, a pass which meets all the other quality criteria will be unsuccessful if the player makes his intentions obvious. "Telegraphing" a pass gives a signal to the opposition as well as your team-mates. The passer can use a range of ploys to disguise his intention. We have already mentioned the value of an unexpected backheeled pass. While this shouldn't be overused, the basic principle of looking at one player and passing to another can be employed in a variety of situations. A whole range of feints and dummies can also be used to disguise a pass. Watch the top players in action and perhaps develop a few tricks of your own! Remember, adding disguise to your passing isn't just a neat trick. Such passes will give the receiver more time on the ball, time that he may use to your team's advantage and the opposition's misfortune.

To sum up

Passing is the key skill in football. It is the means by which individual team members combine for a common purpose: defending one goal and attacking the other. Passing shouldn't be seen in isolation. Good movement is the opposite side of the coin. Young players often make the mistake of making such a good pass that they can't resist stopping to admire it! Good players are on the move as soon as the pass is delivered, looking to support the man in possession and make sure he has plenty of options. Coaches might enthuse over flashes of individual brilliance – a mazy dribble or overhead kick, for example – but these are the icing on the cake. Passing and moving are the lifeblood of every successful team.

Passing is the key skill in football. It is the means by which individual team members combine for a common purpose. It is the most practised aspect of football at every standard throughout the game. Seen here are players from the German national team going through their passing drills in training.

CONTROLLING THE BALL

Ivan Campo of Bolton (left)
and Patrick Viera of Arsenal

Football is a passing game. On average, four out of five times when a player is in possession he will pass the ball. That is only half the story, of course. For every pass that is delivered, another player has to receive it. Ball control can thus be considered as 50 per cent of the passing game.

Creating time and space

A player may sometimes have the luxury of controlling a perfectly weighted and directed pass while in plenty of space. More often he will have to deal with a ball that might be bouncing or spinning awkwardly and with an opponent snapping at his heels. Instant control under pressure is the hallmark of a class player. It is a fine skill to behold and on occasions it can almost be worthy of applause in its own right. Go ahead and applaud if you wish, but you may be in danger of missing the point. Wonderful one-touch control achieves nothing in itself. What it does is give the player valuable extra time on the ball. This has two important advantages. First, it reduces the possibility of a defender getting in a challenge. This is because a player is at his most vulnerable when he is receiving the ball. Instant control thus makes the window of opportunity for the defender as small as possible. Second, good control allows a player to initiate his next move more quickly. Whether he decides to pass himself, run with the ball, dribble or shoot, he will be in a position to do so that little bit sooner. We may only be talking about a fraction of a second, but in a game like football that could be vital. Passing and shooting options can open and close in that time.

Anticipation

The first element of good control is anticipation. Remember that we are not only talking about receiving a deliberate pass from a team-mate. There are also clearances from goalkeepers and defenders, deflections and stray passes from opponents. Anticipating where the ball is heading and getting into line as early as possible are big steps along the way to controlling it.

Continuing the speed of thought theme, you should quickly decide which part of the body you are going to use to control the ball. As well as the feet, the chest and thigh are the contact surfaces which are used most often to receive the ball.

Side of the foot

This is the most used and most effective way of bringing the ball under control. Watch the ball on to the side of your foot then pull the foot back on impact to cushion the ball to the ground in front of you. Practise against a wall, varying the pace and height of the ball as it returns to you.

Controlling the ball

Now you have to decide whether you are going to cushion the ball or use your controlling touch to play it in a particular direction. Generally, in a congested area, cushion control will be needed. This means taking the pace out of the ball by relaxing the contact surface. But killing the ball at your feet is by no means always appropriate. If you are a striker, having the ball stuck between your feet is extremely awkward. Professionals talk about needing an extra touch to "get the ball out of your feet". That extra touch takes time, and a chance might go begging.

In any area of the pitch you should use your first touch to guide the ball in a particular direction, as long as space allows. This could be to set up a dribble or shooting opportunity; it could be simply to shield the ball from an opponent.

Thigh trap

Get into line with the flight of the ball.
Bring your thigh up and on impact, drop it down. Aim to make contact with the ball as high up the thigh as possible. By introducing an element of resistance the ball can be set up for a volley. Conversely, by relaxing the thigh the ball can be dropped at your feet.

Guiding the ball

One of the best examples of using first touch to guide the ball instead of killing it came in the famous England versus Argentina match in the 1998 World Cup. From a deep position, David Beckham played the ball up to Michael Owen, who was near the halfway line. Owen saw that he had space in front of him, so he helped the ball on with the outside of his right boot. A few touches and a few seconds later, the ball was in the back of Argentina's net. Had Owen killed the ball with his first touch he might well have been closed down by a defender and forced to lay it off, and we wouldn't have witnessed one of the best World Cup goals ever scored.

To sum up, good control - and particularly good first touch - is a key skill. It buys time and space, the most important commodities on the football field. And the more time and space a player has, the more likely he is to make his use of the ball count.

Even players renowned for their superb stengths on the ground like David Beckham have also developed good skills for controlling high balls. It is much easier to make penetrating passes when the ball is under full control.

Sole of the foot

Contact is made as the ball hits the ground as the ball is wedged under the foot to stop it bouncing away. Watch the ball carefully. Split second timing is crucial to stop the ball running away from you.

Head control

Using the head to control the ball is a difficult skill. Michael Owen often uses this to good effect to steer the ball in front of him so he can run on to the ball at pace. You should be leaning back slightly, watching the ball on to your forehead and guiding it to the ground.

Chest trap

The chest is a large area on which to catch the ball so there is a good margin of error. It is particularly important to make sure you have read the line of flight because it will be hard to change position after you have set your body to receive the ball. Be on your toes and leaning back slightly when the ball makes contact. You can either decide to cushion the ball or use your controlling touch to play it in a particular direction.

You can take the ball at different heights by bending your knees more.

Firm control

If the ball is travelling very fast there is often no option other than to keep the body solid on impact and guide it down to the ground. Here it is important to get well on top of the ball.

Cushion control

The key point to bear in mind with cushion control is that the part of the body receiving the ball must yield on impact. A rigid, tense surface will cause the ball to rebound away from the body. Practise relaxing the muscles and withdrawing the foot (or thigh or chest) at the point of contact so as to take the pace off the ball.

James Beattie (l) keeps his eyes fixed on the ball even under pressure from Tim Sherwood (r). Always keep your body between your opponent and the ball.

Alan Shearer of Newcastle United.

When your team is in possession, the name of the game is to create as many chances as possible, and put as many of those chances away as you can. Attractive build-up play is all very well, but it's goals that count. And the single most important thing a team can do to maximise its scoring potential is to get as many shots on target as it can. If this sounds obvious, then it is surprising how many teams disregard this advice.

With the responsibility of shooting comes a fear of failure. The ball might hit the corner flag and you might be criticised for not passing to a well-positioned team-mate. This is entirely the wrong attitude. Even the Robbie Fowlers of this world occasionally balloon a shot well over the bar, but that doesn't stop them eagerly awaiting their next shooting opportunity. Unless a player shoots from an impossible distance or angle, he should be encouraged rather than blamed.

Shoot first

So the advice is simple. Make shooting your first thought, and only if the shot isn't on should you consider other options.

Shooting is partly instinctive. Top strikers seem to have an uncanny knack for knowing where the goal is, even if they have their back to the target. Having said that, there are techniques that can be practised and tips that can be followed to improve a player's shooting.

Francesco Totti combines power and accuracy when he shoots.

SHOOTING SKILLS

1. Aim low

Goalkeepers prefer rising shots; it is much easier for them to spring up for a high ball than to get down to a low shot. Also, a low shot might be deflected. And even if it is well off target it might fall invitingly at the feet of a team-mate and turn into an astute pass!

2. Shoot early

Players with poor technique or who are out of form and lacking in confidence often take an extra second and an extra touch to set themselves up for a shot. Dwelling on the ball in this way can result in a lost opportunity. Snap shots pay dividends. They allow defenders less time to get in a challenge, and goalkeepers less time to position themselves.

3. Accuracy or power?

If you imagine the 6-yard box extended to the penalty spot, that forms a rectangle inside which the vast majority of goals are scored. From such a close range, accuracy is more important than power. Much better to pass the ball into the corner of the net than to try a hopeful blast aimed at the centre of the goal. That shouldn't undermine the importance of distance shooting, however. A 25-yard effort might have an element of surprise, and if there is a crowded box, the keeper's view might be obscured. The Brazilians have recognised the value of long-range shooting for many years, with Real Madrid's Roberto Carlos their current thunderbolt specialist. Scoring from distance has helped Brazil to lift the World Cup on a record four occasions. In practice, all shots are a combination of accuracy and power. Even the hardest-struck efforts on goal ought to have a measure of control about them.

Make shooting your first thought

Even off balance Pellegrin of Uruguay gets his shot away. Dwelling on the ball can result in a lost opportunity. Snap shots pay dividends. They allow defenders less time to get in a challenge, and goalkeepers less time to set themselves. So make shooting your first thought, and only if the shot isn't on should you consider other options.

4. Use both feet

We have already mentioned that when it comes to shooting, he who hesitates is lost. Adjusting your body position so that you always strike the ball with your stronger foot may result in a chance going begging. Two-footed players will give defenders and goalkeepers a lot more to think about.

5. Anticipate and gamble

Deflections, flick-ons, rebounds and the like can see the ball pinging around the box at speed. Top strikers seem to develop a knack for knowing where the ball will break, especially in a crowded area. Even if you haven't got the instincts of a Fowler or Solskjaer you should always be alert and ready to pounce on any ball that runs loose in and around the box.

Lorenzo Amoruso shoots with power, but even the hardest-struck efforts on goal ought to have a measure of control about them.

Constant practice

Constant practice allows you to shoot with good technique even under pressure.

HEADING

Christian Correia Dionisio rises to head the ball.

There are two big obstacles to overcome when it comes to heading the ball. The first is fear. When a ball is hurtling towards your face, the natural reaction is to treat it like any other missile. Self-preservation takes over and we want to shield ourselves, duck, turn our head away and close our eyes. To be good in the air, players must learn to suppress these reactions.

Once the fear factor has been overcome, the second hurdle is to master an extremely complex skill. The timing has to be absolutely perfect to meet the ball and send it in the required direction. Doing so while under the pressure of a challenge makes this doubly difficult.

Aerial power

Football purists don't like to see too many high balls and aerial battles. They maintain that the game is meant to be played on the ground, with ball to feet. While there is a lot of truth in this, aerial power has always been an important feature of the British game. Superb headers of the ball such as Teddy Sheringham and Alan Shearer are following in a long tradition of expertise in this aspect of the game. Also, it should be remembered that even the best defenders can't do much about a ball sailing over their heads. The combination of good aerial passes and powerful headers of the ball can be an excellent attacking ploy. Indeed, something like one goal in five is scored from a header. No team can afford to ignore an attacking weapon of such potential.

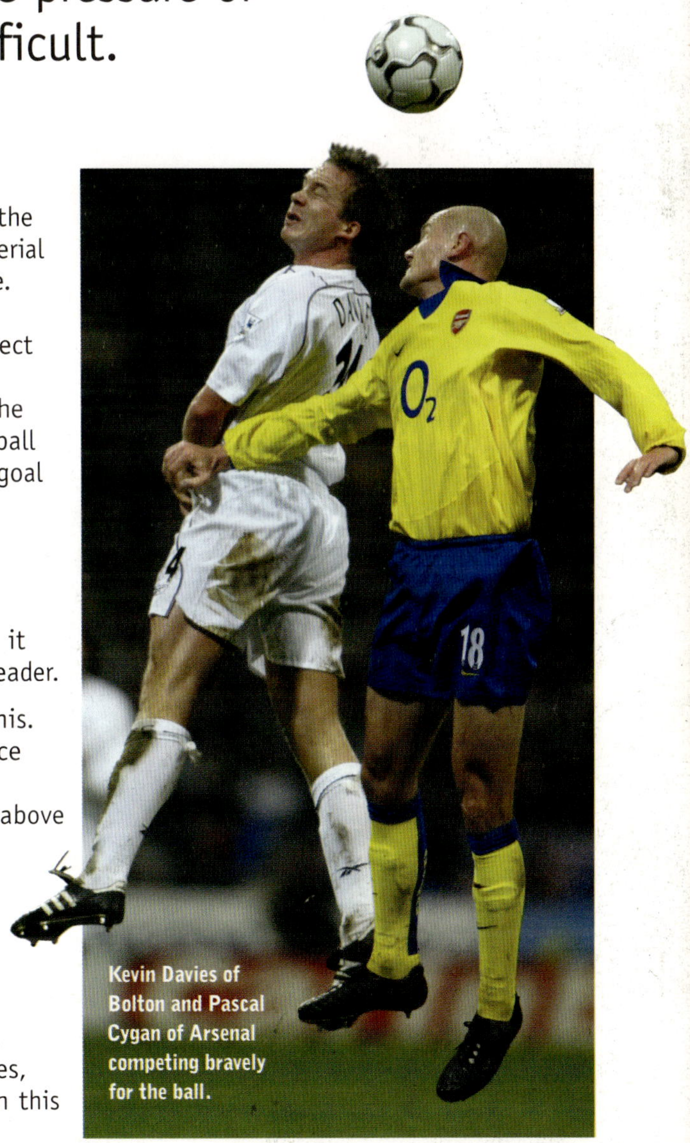

Kevin Davies of Bolton and Pascal Cygan of Arsenal competing bravely for the ball.

Attacking the ball

Let's look at the basic technique for heading the ball, then how it can be applied in different ways to perform different kinds of header.

Meet the ball with the forehead. There are three reasons for this. The skull is at its thickest here, and even a ball travelling at pace won't hurt; the surface is relatively flat, making controlling the direction of header that much easier; and meeting the ball just above eye level will help a player to watch it right up to the point of impact.

Strike the ball, don't let it strike you. It is important to attack the ball with confidence. Holding back and waiting for the ball to arrive is to invite an interception.

Use the back and neck muscles in tandem to generate forward momentum. By punching through the ball using the neck muscles, you will impart maximum power on to the ball. One exception in this regard is the cushioned header, which is discussed later.

DIFFERENT TYPES OF HEADER

1. Defensive header

The priority here is to clear the danger zone, so it is vital to get maximum height, width and distance. You may be giving away possession, but the theory is that if the ball is headed well outside the defensive third, then your team will have the opportunity to get in a good position to win it back in a less dangerous area. Contact with the ball should be made just below the horizontal midline. You certainly don't want to get over the ball and head it downwards, possibly to a striker's feet. And if you get underneath it too much, you will send the ball high into the air but won't get much distance.

If you are deep inside your own area or facing your own goal, then heading the ball out of play for a corner or throw-in might be a better option. Finally, remember that heading the ball back to your goalkeeper does not constitute a backpass. However, great care should be taken, particularly if speedy strikers are on hand to latch on to any underhit ball. If possible, headed backpasses should be cushioned and wide of goal, just to be on the safe side. Cushioned headers will be dealt with separately.

Defensive header

It is vital to get maximum height, width and distance. Contact with the ball should be made just below the horizontal midline.

Practise first

Heading skills should be developed slowly. To begin with, practise getting your timing right with a static ball, perhaps suspended from the crossbar. You can then move on to attacking a moving ball thrown by a partner. The acid test will come in a game situation, when you will have to compete for the ball against real opponents.

Attacking header

1. Timing of the run and jump is important.
2. Contact with the ball should be above the horizontal midline. Get well over the ball to head it down. Arch your back and snap forward at the point of impact.

Emile Mpenza of Belgium meets the ball perfectly with the forehead. The skull is at its thickest here, and even a ball travelling at pace won't hurt.

2. Attacking header

Accuracy is obviously far more important here. With a goal measuring just eight yards by eight feet, the attacker has a much smaller target area than a defender clearing his lines. And with a goalkeeper to beat, the attacker can't afford to sacrifice too much power either. The attacker's first priority must be to get ahead of the defender and get to the ball first. The timing of the run, and also the jump if required, must be spot on.

If you are in a fairly central position relative to the goal, you have the choice of directing your header towards the near or far post. If you are at the far post, you will be powering the ball back the way it has come, either trying to beat the keeper at his near post or heading the ball back across the face of goal towards the far post.

3. Glancing header

If you are in front of the near post, or if the ball is played into the box from a deep position, then a glancing header will be needed. Here, you are using the forehead to redirect the ball. A fuller contact will be required if you are aiming for the near post, a more delicate contact if you're going for the far post. You can't generate much power with a glancing header; most of the pace on the ball comes from the delivery. Judging the angle of deflection off the forehead is not easy. Only experience and practice will help you develop a feel for the kind of contact required.

4. The flick on

A variation of the glancing header is the flick on. Here, the attacker allows the ball to skim off the forehead or top of the head. Many teams use this tactic at corner kicks. One attacker flicks the ball on at the near post, while his team-mates time their runs to arrive at the far post area. Defenders can be caught out by the change of direction on the ball, whereas the attacking side has the advantage of being able to anticipate such a delivery.

Finally, remember that when you go for goal with a header, a low ball will cause most problems for the goalkeeper. To direct the ball downwards you must get over it, making contact above the horizontal midline.

Frank Lampard using his forehead to redirect the ball. A fuller contact will be required if you are aiming for the near post, a more delicate contact if you're going for the far post. For a strong deflection, twist the body with the head. This will mean you end up facing the direction in which you want the ball to go.

5. Cushioned header

If you are using a header to pass to a team-mate or back to the goalkeeper, the normal rules for all passing still apply. That means putting the ball in an area and at a pace that will help the receiver to control the ball comfortably. He certainly won't thank you for a bullet header coming straight at him from five yards! This is when the cushioned header comes into its own. Just as you withdraw your foot to take the pace off a ball played along the ground, so you allow your head to "give" for a ball played in the air. By relaxing your neck and back muscles, your forehead absorbs power instead of generating it, and the result should be a nicely weighted pass for your team-mate.

A cushioned header can be just as effective in attack. If a cross has come in to the penalty area with too much pace because the winger was under pressure the same technique can be used to loop the ball into the net rather than power it over the bar.

Paul Scholes heads for goal.

Sheer power - Zinedine Zidane scores against Brazil in the 1998 World Cup. Two of the three goals which brought France victory came from the head of Zidane. One goal in five is scored from a header. No team can afford to ignore an attacking weapon of such potential.

TURNING AND DRIBBLING

Dennis Bergkamp of Arsenal
takes control of the ball.

There is no better sight in football than a player with the ball seemingly tied to his feet, taking on defender after defender and leaving them beaten and bewildered. In a tight game involving two well-drilled defences, players might struggle to find the time and space necessary to create goalscoring opportunities. In these kind of games the dribbling artists can really come into their own.

Creating space

Once a player goes past an opponent, he opens up space for himself. Another defender will be forced to come and challenge, even if that means leaving the player he is marking. In short, the whole defence can quickly unravel if a clever dribbler can take one or two players out of the game.

Bastia's defender Pascal Chimbonda (l) vies with Nantes's striker Hassan Ahamada.

Mesmerising dribble

One of the best goals ever scored came after a mesmerising dribble from the great Diego Maradona. It happened in the quarter-finals of the 1986 World Cup, when England came up against Argentina. Maradona scored both goals in Argentina's victory. He punched the ball into the net for the first, but the second goal was pure magic. He ran half of the length of the pitch and beat half the England team before slotting the ball into the net. Twelve years later, at France 98, the two teams met again. This time it was Michael Owen who scored a wonder goal. Owen picked up the ball in a similar position to Maradona but he evaded the defenders more through blistering pace than marvellous footwork.
Young players tend to watch the tricks that players like Maradona and Owen use to beat defenders. However, most go on to develop their own style. With dribbling techniques, there are no hard and fast rules. If it works, use it. Having said that, although players such as Craig Bellamy, Michael Owen and Ryan Giggs might appear very different in style, they all use variations on the same basic ideas. Let's look at some of them.

DRIBBLING

Good close control is vital

Ideally, the ball should remain within playing distance at all times. There will be exceptions, of course. If a lot of space has opened up in front of you, or if sheer pace is your main weapon, then playing the ball further away from your body might be appropriate.

Not all good dribblers are speed merchants

In fact, change of gear can be just as effective as out-and-out pace. A player like Paul Gascoigne regularly beats players with excellent close control and quick bursts of acceleration over 10 or 15 yards.

Changes of direction can be just as disconcerting for defenders as changes of pace

By twisting and turning, the attacker will force the defender into adjusting his stride pattern and body position. Cristiano Ronaldo does this probably better than anybody. Defenders are frequently left back-pedalling and off balance, sometimes struggling to stay on their feet, never mind make a tackle!

Vary which part of the boot makes contact with the ball

The inside and outside of both feet give four basic contact surfaces. Dragbacks using the soles of the feet give two more. The more variety you have in your dribbling technique, the more unsettling it will be for defenders.

Use feints and dummies

There are any number of ways to introduce these into your dribbling technique. One of the most basic is to step over or arc around the ball with one foot, then play it in the opposite direction with the other. Emile Heskey and Steve McManaman both favour this trick. It is surprising that even when a defender knows what might be coming, it still works nearly every time if well executed.

Protect the ball

If you keep your body between the ball and the chasing defender, he will find it difficult to tackle cleanly.

Cristiano Ronaldo of Manchester United tussles with Paul Konchesky of Tottenham.

Dropping the shoulder

1 Here the attacking player runs towards the defender, transferring his body weight to his left so that it looks as if he is going to move in that direction. An exaggerated drop of the shoulder helps to convince the defender of his intentions.

2 The defender moves to intercept and has already begun to commit himself when the attacker changes direction. With the defender's body weight on his right leg, the attacking player accelerates past him on the opposite side.

Play with your head up

You should keep your eye on the ball when you're playing it, but between touches you should glance up and be aware of how the play is developing around you. Even top players can be at fault in this regard. David Ginola is a masterful dribbler, but has often been criticised for the lack of end product to his work. Beating three players only to be dispossessed by the fourth may be highly entertaining but it is of little value to the team.

Don't be afraid of failure

Providing you are not deep inside your own territory - where the risks outweigh the benefits - take your opponent on with confidence. As with shooting, after several unsuccessful attempts you might hit the jackpot with the next. A player deserves more applause for trying to beat his man than for taking the soft option of a negative pass.

Alessandro Del `Piero during training. Develop your ability to turn quickly by running slalom style through posts or any markers. This will also build up your quadriceps and improve your speed over short distances.

The step-over

❶ ❷ The attacker makes as if to play the ball with the outside of his left foot.
❸ ❹ Instead, he swings his foot over the ball and plants it on the ground.
❺ He pushes off this foot and goes past his opponent on the right, playing the ball with his right foot as he does so.

Good technique

In summary, although the emphasis in the modern game is on passing and moving, dribbling skills can open up the tightest defences. All players should work on their technique; dribbling isn't just for flying wingers.

Finally, it ought to be said that even unsuccessful dribbles can reap rewards. That is because dribbling often results in a set play. Good tackles frequently knock the ball out for a throw-in or corner; foul tackles lead to direct free kicks or penalties. As so many goals come from set pieces, it can be said that dribbling contributes both directly and indirectly towards creating scoring opportunities.

TURNING

Before you can dribble you have to make space for yourself. Often you will have your back to a defender which means you either have to play the ball back to a team-mate or turn and beat your marker.

If you are near your own goal you should show greater caution and play the way you are facing. However, in the attacking third, there are advantages to turning and trying to go past your marker. If you pass him you can take him out of the game, but even if you only make some space for yourself a shooting opportunity can arise.

Marcel Rath (front) and Pal Dardai. When the defender is tight against you this could be the opportunity to spin off him and accelerate away.

Peter van der Heyden shields the ball from Latvia's Imants Bleidelis. While shielding the ball, try to watch your opponent's movements with your peripheral vision. This will help you to decide which way to turn.

Vladimir Smicer of Liverpool buys time by shielding the ball from Roy Keane of Manchester United.

Turning while closely marked

1. Keep your body between your opponent and the ball and use your body strength against the defender as he pushes into you. Good balance is essential.

2. You can screen the ball to block any attempt by your opponent to get round you. Keep the ball close to you. When the player is right up against your back this could be the opportunity to turn against him. This needs to be timed perfectly. You must turn just at the time he tries to come around your side to make a challenge.

If the ball is well away from your body, beyond your playing distance, blocking an opponent in this way would be deemed obstruction and result in a free kick. You can only shield the ball when it is in your possession.

Ruud van Nistelrooy uses his body to obscure William Gallas's view of the ball. This will give van Nistelrooy an advantage when he decides which way he will turn.

TACKLING AND DEFENDING

Manchester United's Christiano Ronaldo.

TACKLING

If the opposition has the ball, you can gain possession in one of two ways. One is the direct method, the tackle. The other way is by taking up good defensive positions, denying time and space, pressurising the man on the ball and forcing a mistake. Tackling is thus just one aspect of the defender's art. Let's look at tackling techniques, and then at the broader subject of defending.

The golden rule

The golden rule is to tackle when you are sure of winning the ball; otherwise, jockey the attacker and bide your time.

There are exceptions, of course. A striker in an advanced position might take a chance with a tackle, knowing that there is potentially a rich reward if it is successful, and little risk if he fails to win the ball. Also, a defender can't back off and jockey indefinitely! If he's retreating into his box, or an attacker is through on goal, then a defender might have to commit to a tackle whatever the circumstances.

Timing

A player is at his most vulnerable when he is receiving the ball, and this is the best time to make a tackle. Once he has it under control, take a more cautious approach. Keep your eye on the ball, not on any fancy footwork or body feints. On the other hand, if you feint to tackle, it might force a mistake from the attacker. Wait for the moment that the ball is beyond his playing distance, then make your move.

Once you have decided to commit to a tackle, the key factors are speed, determination, accuracy and timing. All of these are necessary if you are going to win the ball cleanly and not commit a foul.

A defender can't back off and jockey indefinitely but you can only tackle legitimately when you are alongside your opponent. Here Poland's Pawel Kryszatowicz slides in to tackle Wales' Mark Pembridge. If contact is made with the player's legs before contact with the ball, a foul is committed.

Whoever gets more foot on the ball and drives through the challenge with their body weight is likely to win the ball.

Block tackle

The block tackle is the most common challenge in football, and can be made from the front or side. In the front-on tackle, you should place your standing foot beside the ball and drive through the challenge with your body weight behind the tackling leg. Contact is made with the side of the foot through the middle of the ball.

The side-on block tackle occurs when the attacker and defender are side-by-side rather than facing each other. The tackler gets as close as possible, then pivots on his standing leg, bringing the tackling foot round to make contact with the ball, using the same side-foot technique.

Although only the foot makes contact with the ball, the whole body makes the tackle. Approach the tackle as if making a side-foot pass and meet the ball solidly with the side of the foot. A low, well-balanced body will give the most chance of success.

Here, player 1 has more foot in contact with the ball because he is using the side of his foot and is therefore likely to win the challenge.

Player 2 is attempting to win the ball with the power of his instep, where there is less surface area in contact with the ball.
Timing is important. Be committed to the tackle. It only hurts if you pull out of it at the last moment.

Slide tackle

The slide tackle is a challenge of total commitment, since you are out of the game for a few precious moments if you don't win the ball. In fact, the basic rule is to stay on your feet whenever possible. However, slide tackles do allow defenders to make up valuable extra ground, and perhaps enable a player to reach the ball earlier than if he took an extra stride. If a defender is chasing a player who is through on goal, that fraction of a second gained by making a slide tackle could be the difference between getting in a challenge or not.

Most slide tackles are made from the side or from behind. In the latter case in particular, the tackler must ensure he makes contact with the ball first, not the attacker's leg, or he will concede a free kick. Ideally, the tackle should be made with the leg furthest away from the ball. In practice, many players tackle with their strongest leg, no matter which side of the attacker they are on.

The slide tackle is often used simply to dispossess an opponent or put the ball out of play. However, if the timing is perfect, it can be used to win possession. Instead of making firm contact with the ball, the tackler hooks his foot around it, cradling it on his instep. The attacker's momentum will carry him forward, leaving the tackler free to get up with the ball at his feet.

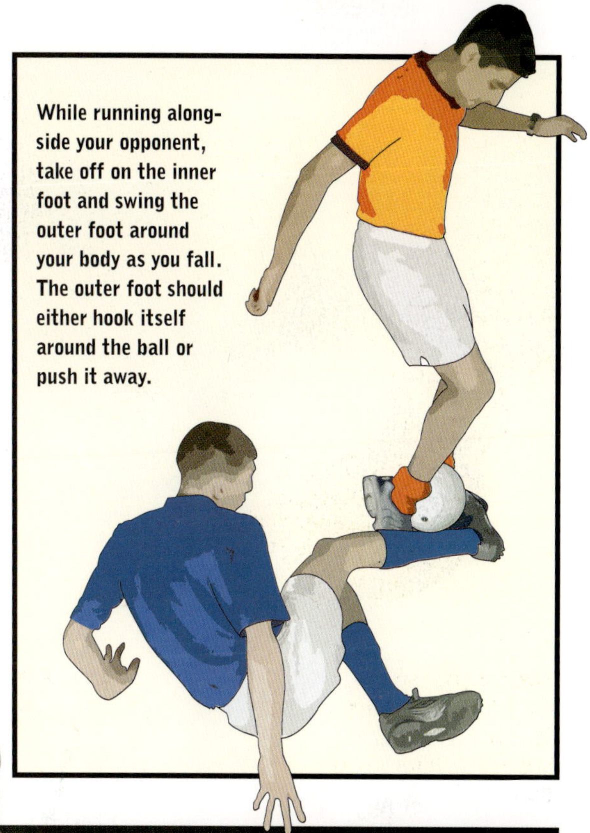

While running alongside your opponent, take off on the inner foot and swing the outer foot around your body as you fall. The outer foot should either hook itself around the ball or push it away.

El Hadji Diouf making a slide tackle on John O'Shea. The slide tackle is a challenge of total commitment, since you are out of the game for a few precious moments if you don't win the ball. If in doubt, stay on your feet.

Thai Yuthajak Konjan (centre) tries to escapes from Laos' Vixay Phaphouvanin (left). Very often a defender can cause problems for his team by tackling and failing to win the ball. If the attacker chooses to dribble, the defender should not commit himself. The tactic should be to jockey and harry, and, if possible, force your opponent towards the touchline or square across the pitch. Only tackle when you are convinced you can win the ball.

DEFENDING

The team in possession of the ball is the attacking team; the team without the ball is the defending team. There are no half measures, and it doesn't matter what number is on your shirt.

The aim of the defending side is to win the ball. As we have seen, this can be achieved by tackling. However, attackers are becoming increasingly wily and clever at shielding the ball; and referees are becoming increasingly quick to clamp down on the slightest mistimed challenge. For these reasons, many teams simply opt to make life as difficult as possible for the attacking side. Instead of tackling, the defending team concentrates on getting players goal-side, then putting pressure on the man in possession. By closing him down and denying him time and space, the defending side exerts a lot of pressure. The player on the ball might be forced into a negative pass, a risky forward pass or a dribble. If he opts to pass, it could be misdirected - offering the possibility of an interception. Alternatively if the receiver is also immediately put under pressure, he might miscontrol the ball.

If the attacker chooses to dribble, the defender should not commit himself. Again, the tactic should be to jockey and harry, and, if possible, force your opponent towards the touchline or square across the pitch.

Note that defending in this way requires good movement and positional play, with every outfield player helping to crank up the pressure on the attacking side. There is no technique involved until the defending side forces a mistake and manages to intercept or make a tackle.

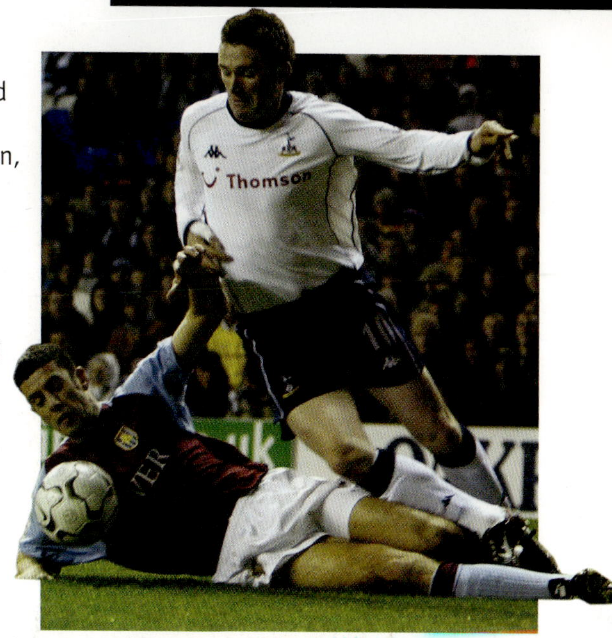

Mark Delaney tackles Robbie Keane. Ideally a slide tackle or interception should be made with the leg furthest away from the ball.

In practice, many players tackle with their strongest leg, no matter which side of the attacker they are on.

Paul Telfer of Southampton tackles Frederic Kanoute of Tottenham Hotspur but still retains possession. Once a defender has committed a tackle but has failed to win the ball he is briefly out of the game.

GOALKEEPING

AC Milan's Ukraine forward Andriy Shevchenko (l) fights for a ball with Boca Juniors goalkeeper Roberto Carlos Abbondanzieri.

The goalkeeper is the single most important member of the team. Outfield players might have technical weaknesses, play badly or even "hide" on the pitch. After a game, few people remember such individual performances, especially if the game has been won. And even if they do remember a poor individual display by an outfield player, it can be hard to relate it to the final score.

These luxuries aren't open to the goalkeeper. There is nowhere to hide, and any blunders or flaws in his technique usually result in him picking the ball out of the back of his net.

On the positive side, goalkeepers can win games just as well as prolific strikers. Coaches often talk about a team needing a strong spine, and that starts with the goalkeeper. Coaches know that a top-class 'keeper can be worth 10 points per season to a side. The dividing line between success and failure is so narrow that a quality goalkeeper can make the crucial difference.

What makes a good goalkeeper?

Goalkeepers are usually tall; they certainly must be a dominant physical presence in order to command their box and instil confidence in the defence. 'Keepers need to be agile and athletic, with excellent reflexes and hand-eye coordination. And as far as physical attributes are concerned, let's not forget a good pair of hands!

Goalkeepers have to be brave, prepared to go for the ball when attackers' boots might be flying. They must be cool when they are under pressure, and able to maintain high levels of concentration when they're not. Finally, between the sticks is no place to be if you are a shrinking violet! Communication is vital, and in the heat of the game that usually means bawling at the top of your voice. Watch David James or Peter Schmeichel in action and you'll see how clearly they make their views known to their team-mates! This is very important, as the 'keeper is often well placed to spot any danger signals and marshal his defence to deal with them.

Taking the ball palms down with eyes fixed on the ball.

SHOT STOPPING

The range of shots that a 'keeper has to deal with is almost endless. They fire in at different heights and from different angles. One attacker might go for sheer power, another clever placement. The ball can dip or swerve. And if that's not enough, there are the extra uncertainties of being unsighted, bobbles off the turf and deflections off players. Nevertheless, there are some basic principles which 'keepers should heed when dealing with shots.

- **Be alert and on your toes** - quite literally. The ideal position is on an imaginary line between the ball and the centre of the goal-line. This line obviously changes as the ball travels across the field and the 'keeper should adjust his position accordingly.
- **Keep your eye on the ball.** If an attacker is shaping to shoot, don't be distracted by anything else that is going on.
- **Get as much of your body as possible** behind the ball. Ideally, take the ball with both hands, with the body behind as a secondary barrier. If there is time, move your body into position instead of diving.
- **Sideways steps.** If you do have time to move across your goal, use sideways steps; don't cross your legs.
- **Two hands are better than one.** If you can't get your body behind the ball, two hands are better than one. Spread the fingers of both hands behind the ball and bring it into the body as soon as possible.
- **Catch if you can**, punch if you are in any doubt. If you do opt to punch, go for height and distance, and put the ball out on to the flanks rather than down the middle of the pitch. For a shot dipping under the bar or just inside the post, a one-handed deflection is often needed. Use the palms of the hands to guide the ball over the bar or round the post. Conceding a corner is better than conceding a goal.

Ideally the goalkeeper should take the ball with both hands, with his body behind as a secondary barrier. If there is time, move your body into position instead of diving. The knees should be bent and legs apart to achieve a good base for balance.

When diving, push off on the leg nearest the ball

Maintain a sideways position through the air. It is easy to twist into a face-down position, and if that happens you won't be able to watch the ball.

When making a save, relax the part of the body that meets the ball

This will have a cushioning effect and make the possibility of a rebound less likely.

Sometimes goalkeepers need a bit of good luck

They may dive the wrong way and make a save with a trailing leg. It doesn't look pretty but it's just as effective as an elegant, swan-like dive. These kind of saves are often not as fortunate as they appear. The 'keeper is usually making himself as big a target as possible, increasing the chances of the ball hitting him. In any case, goalkeepers have such a hard job that they deserve the odd stroke of good fortune.

Czech Sparta Prague goalkeeper Jaromir Blazek clasps the ball to his chest. Many 'keepers take the ball in the stomach area by diving towards it with the arms folded in behind to secure it.

One-on-one situations

We have already looked at how a goalkeeper should move across his goal, depending on the position of the ball. If an attacker is through on goal, he must also be ready to move forward. Coming out to meet the attacker will give the latter a much smaller target to aim at. This is known as narrowing the angle.

Advancing from the goal-line does bring dangers, however. If the 'keeper goes too far or not far enough, too early or too late, the attacker will have the upper hand. Depending on the 'keeper's position, the striker could shoot low, go for a chip, dribble or pass to a team-mate. The 'keeper should advance when the ball is beyond the attacker's playing distance. When the attacker has the ball under control, the 'keeper should check his run and take up a ready position.

For a ball at chest or head height

Here you can see Kasey Keller (left) and Edwin van der Sar (above) catching high balls. There comes a point when it is better to take the ball with the palms up. This is when the ball has risen to chest height or higher. The hands should give on impact, so the ball doesn't bounce away. You may need to jump to get well behind the ball.

Stay on your feet

Try to force the attacker wide, on to his weaker foot, or both. Don't go to ground too early; make yourself look as big as possible, perhaps with arms flailing to try to put the attacker off. When you do decide to go for the ball, wait for a moment when the attacker is looking at the ball or when it is beyond his playing distance. Spread yourself wide as you go down. If you don't manage to get the ball, you might have forced the attacker into a more difficult position from which to score, and perhaps gained time for your defenders to recover.

Fabien Barthez makes a save low to his right. He collapses the leg nearest to the ball and takes the ball with the palms down.

Diving

When diving, push off on the leg nearest the ball. Always try to maintain a sideways position through the air. It is easy to twist into a face-down position, and if that happens you won't be able to watch the ball. Take the ball with the palms down.

Arsenal's goalkeeper Jens Lehmann claims the ball.

Always try and get two hands to the ball even when diving at full length.

DEALING WITH CROSSES

Relatively few attacks come straight through the middle, where the defence is strongest. More often, a team will attack down the flanks and put the ball into the box from wide positions. Dealing with these crosses is a key skill for a goalkeeper.

Taking up a good starting position is important. If the attacker is out wide, the 'keeper should be in the centre of the goal or slightly nearer the far post. It is easier to go forward than to back-pedal. If the attacker cuts in, the 'keeper should move towards the near post. For angled crosses from further out, the keeper should maintain a central position but advance to the 6-yard line.

When the ball is in flight, the goalkeeper must decide whether to go for it or not. The decision will be based mainly on the pace and trajectory of the ball, but the number of bodies that are in the way will also be a factor. Once his mind is made up, the 'keeper should be decisive. He should attack the ball at speed. A one-footed take-off will help to give maximum height, and the 'keeper should take the ball at the highest possible point.

Decide whether you are going to catch or punch early on, and stick to it. Punching will be safer in a crowded area or if you are back-pedalling. If you're not 100% confident of catching the ball, opt to punch. Try to gain maximum height and distance, and put the ball on to the flanks by preference.

- **Once your mind is made up, be decisive.**
- **Attack the ball at speed.**
- **A one-footed take-off will help to give maximum height.**
- **Take the ball at the highest possible point.**
- **Decide whether you are going to catch or punch early on, and stick to it.**
- **Punching will be safer in a crowded area or if you are back-pedalling.**
- **If you're not 100% confident of catching ball, opt to punch.**
- **Try to gain maximum height and distance, and put the ball on to the flanks by preference.**

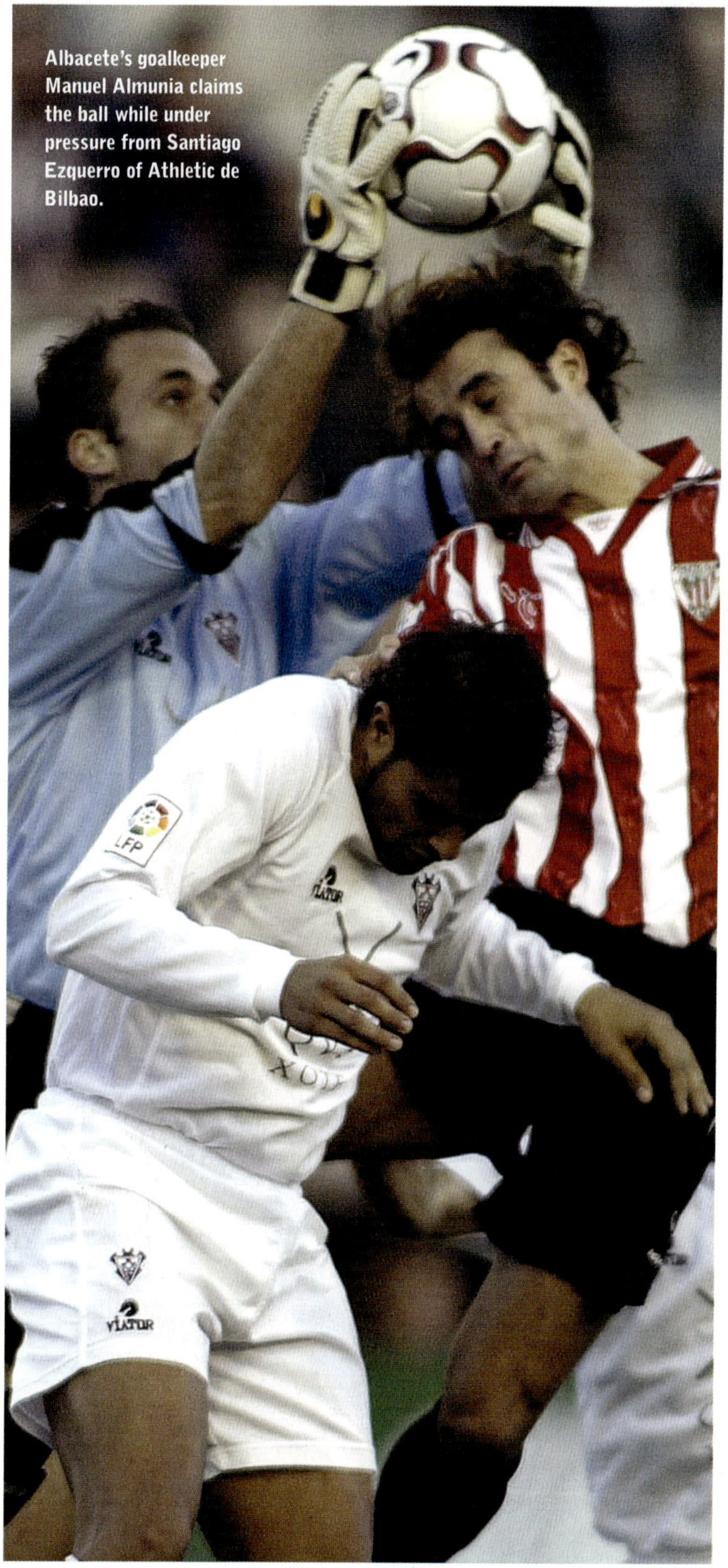
Albacete's goalkeeper Manuel Almunia claims the ball while under pressure from Santiago Ezquerro of Athletic de Bilbao.

The goalkeeper as sweeper and attacker

The best 'keepers think and act like sweepers. They are always alert to balls played into space behind the defence. If the 'keeper can get to the ball first, he might be saving himself from a dangerous one-on-one situation.

The 'keeper's role in launching attacks is also important these days. Once he has the ball in his hands, quick, accurate distribution - either from a throw or kick - can be very effective in setting up counter-attacks.

Tipping the ball over the bar

If the ball is too high to catch or too risky to punch, then tip it over the bar. Stretch as far as you can with one hand to give greater height and use an open palm to deflect the ball over the bar.

Ball on the ground

This is the hardest save to make - that's why strikers keep the ball low. How you make the save will depend on how close the ball is to your body. If the ball is coming close to you, fall on to the ball. If it is slightly further away, collapse the nearest leg. The priority is to get the hands to the ground to meet the ball as quickly as possible. The body can follow on. Here Dimitar Ivankov is stretching for a shot along the ground that was far to his right. His legs are still in the air, almost as if he has dived into a swimming pool.

DEVELOPING SKILLS

Italy's Marco Delvecchio on the training ground.

FREESTYLE FUN

Practice usually comes with a clear purpose. We have looked at all the key footballing skills, with the purpose of making you a better player and increasing your all-round knowledge of the game. But there are some skills that you are unlikely to be able to use during a match.

The basic skill of balancing the ball on your foot will give a feeling of confidence and make you increasingly comfortable with the ball.

Trying to master a trick will improve your overall feel for the ball. Moving the ball as shown in this sequence from the forehead to the back of the neck is one of the more advanced skills.

Basic juggling skills:

- Juggling the ball
- Trying to hold the ball on the instep or back of the neck
- Running towards a stationary ball and trying to flick it up and over your head

Tricks such as these are all good fun. Indeed, before and after practice sessions, all players love to have a go at their favourite party pieces. Do they matter? Should you bother with them? Yes, most definitely! Trying to master a trick or two is valuable for two reasons. First, it gives you the chance to express yourself and have some fun before the serious practice gets under way, or after it has finished. Second, it will improve your overall feel for the ball. There is an old footballing adage which says you should "make friends with the ball". What better way to build up a close friendship than to play around with it in this way? You may not be able to use these exact tricks in a game situation, but they will improve your overall touch and control - and you'll certainly need those skills.

TACTICS

SET PLAYS

Senegal's Makhtar Ndiaye takes a corner kick.

Statistics show that set pieces are the single most productive source of goals. Nearly half of all goals are scored either directly or indirectly from dead-ball situations: free kicks, corners, throw-ins and penalties.

If this figure seems high, then you have to bear in mind the in-built advantages to the attacking side when they have a set play. First, the ball is still, either on the ground or in the hand.

A stationary ball is easier to play than a moving one. Second, the player on the ball cannot be challenged and is therefore under no pressure as he prepares to kick or throw. Third, teams can practise set plays on the training ground. Every player knows what starting position to take up, when and where to move, and - most importantly where the ball is going to be played. The defending side will obviously retreat in numbers, but they have the disadvantage of having to cover every eventuality as an equal threat. Several defenders will be occupied in marking players who know in advance that they are there to create confusion, not to receive the ball.

Attacking play

Occasionally, teams actively try to win set pieces and and thus benefit from all the above advantages. For example, a player in a wide position and heavily marked might deliberately try to play the ball off an opponent's legs to win a corner. More commonly, however, set plays tend to be a very useful by-product of good attacking play. Defenders (including goalkeepers) often concede set pieces when they are under pressure. It follows that if an attacking side can ratchet up the pressure, then the set pieces will come. Pressurising defenders involves running at them, dribbling round them and passing the ball through them and beyond them. As far as goalkeepers are concerned, the best way to put pressure on them is to keep them busy, and that means plenty of crosses and shots.

One final word of caution: because teams can practise set pieces at leisure, they sometimes make them very elaborate affairs. This is a mistake. Over-complicating a set play by involving too many players and too many touches just multiplies the chances of it going wrong. Simplicity is always the best policy.

David Beckham prepares to take a throw-in.

PENALTIES

One situation guaranteed to crank up the tension level is the penalty kick. Countless games have been decided on a converted or missed penalty. Shoot-outs are now the norm for settling drawn matches in all the big tournaments. This has made penalty-taking an important skill for all players, not just the team's spot-kick specialist.

Good technique

The England team has come in for a lot of criticism in recent years, after being knocked out of several tournaments on penalties. Some commentators were amazed to discover that many international players spent little or no time practising their penalty-taking technique. The argument against practising penalties is that the skill won't transfer from the training ground to the heat of battle. Some say it is impossible to re-create the pressure of taking a vital penalty in an important game. There is obviously some truth in this. Penalty-taking is certainly as much about ice-cool temperament as good technique. After all, the onus is on the player to score. Penalties were introduced as a way of punishing the offending side and giving the team awarded the kick an easy goal. Nothing is that easy, however. The 'keeper can position himself slightly off-centre in the goal, wave his arms about, and these days he can even move across his line as the kicker takes his run-up. All these things are aimed at putting off the penalty-taker. If they work, the 'keeper takes the credit; if they fail, he gets no criticism. In other words, the 'keeper can't really lose. It is the kicker who has all the problems. He is expected to score, and that only serves to stoke up the pressure.

Italy's Francesco Toldo dives to save a penalty. Whichever method you prefer, make up your mind what you are going to do and stick to it. Always be ready to follow up a penalty. Most penalty saves are parries, so there is often a second chance to score.

Steve Brown takes a penalty against Maik Taylor. Some penalty-takers go for sheer power using the instep; others prefer good placement using a side-foot technique.

Power or placement

Some penalty-takers go for sheer power using the instep; others prefer good placement using a side-foot technique. There are two dangers with the first method: one is blasting the ball wide, the other is hitting the goalkeeper. Those who go for good placement have a different problem. Because there is less pace on the ball they are naturally keen to put it in the corner of the net. In an effort to ensure that they hit the ball beyond the 'keeper's reach these players sometimes put it the wrong side of the post.

Whichever method you prefer, the watchword is determination: make up your mind what you are going to do, and stick to it. Hesitation or indecision is fatal. There are some players who actually decide not to decide! Their game-plan is to wait until the very last moment, perhaps throw a little shimmy or dummy, wait for the goalkeeper to react and then stroke the ball into the empty net. This is a dangerous form of brinkmanship. If the 'keeper gambles and commits himself early, this method can work very well. But some 'keepers stand their ground to the very last second, waiting for the kicker to commit himself. In effect, it can become a cat-and-mouse game as to who is going to make the first move.

Decisive and confident

The best advice remains to be decisive and confident. Try to block out any peripheral movement or noise on the part of the goalkeeper, other players or supporters. And remember, there is no such thing as a good or bad penalty, only one that ends up in the back of the net and one that doesn't.

FREE KICKS

Set pieces are the richest source of goals, and free kicks produce more goals than any other set play. If you consider those two statements together, the implication is clear: free kicks make a major contribution to a team's goal tally.

This is not quite the complete picture, though. The scoring ratio from free kicks increases significantly at the higher levels of the game. Fewer goals are scored in this way in the junior ranks. Nevertheless, today's juniors are tomorrow's senior players, and there is nothing wrong with youngsters working on techniques and ploys for free kicks in the attacking third. Even if these skills don't pay dividends immediately, they may do so in the future.

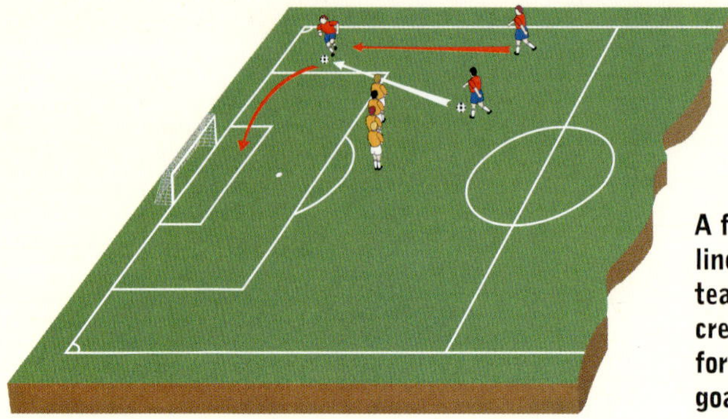

A free kick down the line to an overlapping team-mate can create a good angle for attacking the goal.

When the angle is too acute for a shot, improving the angle by passing the ball centrally is a useful option. While this area is always well defended, it often gives an opportunity for a first-time strike on goal.

US player Ned Grabavoy takes a free-kick against South Korea.

SV Werder Bremen against VFB Stuttgart. Defenders hate having forwards in or around the defensive wall; it can lead to a lot of distracting pushing and shoving which can result in gaps appearing in the wall.

The defensive wall

How many players form a defensive wall will depend on distance, angle to the goal, the reputation of the striker (if known) and the goalkeeper's preference.

Going for goal

Players at all levels of the game are well advised to keep free kicks as simple as possible. A direct strike on goal is the simplest free kick of all. As this involves just one player and one touch, there is less chance of things going astray. Of course, the taker might fluff his kick, but at least the attacking side is ensuring itself a strike on goal. Involving too many players and touches may well mean the move breaks down before it reaches the player who is going to shoot.

Obviously, going for goal is only an option with a direct free kick in a fairly central position just outside the box. For indirect free kicks, or those from deeper or wider positions, then at least two players and two touches will be needed. The possibilities here are endless. Depending on the exact position, you could set up a team-mate to shoot, float the ball into the box, chip it beyond the last defender for a team-mate to run on to, or play a low, slide-rule pass through the defence. Once again, the decision should be based on the capabilities of the individual players.

CORNERS

In open play, teams recognise the value of getting to the by-line before delivering the ball into the box. By doing so, the attacking side has the advantage of meeting a ball coming on to it. Defenders and goalkeepers often struggle to deal with crosses that are moving away from them. Corner kicks have this potential, and much more. In fact, the corner-taker has several options at his disposal. He can swing the ball into the goal or away from it; he can put the ball to the near post, the centre of the goal or the far post; he can drive the ball to the edge of the box for an incoming volleyer; or he can work a short corner with a team-mate.

Any or all of these can be performed on agreed signals. However, don't try to make every corner different just for the sake of it. Most teams tend to have two or three variations. Which ones you specialise in must be decided by looking at your team's strengths and/or the opposition's weaknesses. For example, if you have some powerful headers of the ball, then the

An outswinging corner

The Korean Republic's Ki Bok Seo takes a corner. The approach to the ball is from behind the touchline. This will draw the ball towards the penalty spot for the strikers to run on to. If you have some powerful headers of the ball, then the outswinger aimed towards the penalty spot will be a good option.

outswinger aimed around the penalty spot will be a good stock delivery. On the other hand, if the opposition 'keeper tends to flap at balls played just underneath his crossbar, then inswingers into this area could pay dividends. If you find a formula that works, stick with it.

Remember that a corner is also a pass. The corner-taker may not be able to pick out a particular individual, but he can aim for a specific, pre-arranged target area where he expects one or more of his team-mates to be. The attacking players should try to find space at the critical moment, just as they would for any other kind of pass. They can do this by switching positions and using feints and dummies to make life difficult for the markers.

An inswinging corner

The approach to the ball is from behind the goal-line to give the ball the required sidespin, drawing it in towards the goal. If the opposition 'keeper tends to flap at balls played just underneath his crossbar, then inswingers into this area could pay dividends. They are also potent weapons when delivered short to the near post so they can be flicked on. This late change of trajectory makes it difficult for defenders and goalkeepers to clear.

THROW-INS

Taking a throw-in

- Both feet must be behind the line.
- Both feet must be in contact with the ground at all times.
- Take the ball right behind your head before releasing. The ball must be thrown, not pushed.

Defender Danielle Slaton of the USA does a throw-in, keeping both feet behind the line.

Throw-ins should be regarded in the same light as any other kind of pass. First, you are aiming to retain possession. Also, you should try to make life as easy as possible for the receiver. As with any other pass, sometimes a throw to a team-mate's feet is the right option, sometimes a ball thrown into space is a better choice.

In the attacking third, teams are now more aware of the potential of throw-ins to set up goalscoring chances. Many teams have a long-throw expert who can not only reach the goalmouth, but can do so with greater accuracy than with a corner. Even if you can't achieve such distances, you can increase the attacking threat by bearing the following points in mind.

Gaining an advantage

Get the ball back into play quickly. Defending teams are prone to losing concentration at throw-ins, partly because they are so common. Defences tend to be more worried about corners and free kicks; they often underestimate the potential danger of a throw-in. Take the throw quickly, and you will take maximum advantage if any defenders have "switched off".

Obviously, the one exception to this rule is if you have a long-throw specialist. In that case, there could be a delay while he comes across to take the throw and other players get into position in and around the box.

Alessandro Del Piero (inset) and Bixente Lizarazu. A long follow-through from a ball taken well back behind the head will generate more power for a long throw.

FORMATIONS

The way in which the outfield players line up is a key element in a team's overall tactical approach to the game. Naturally, coaches have experimented with various formations and systems in an effort to improve performances and results. Neither a particular formation nor a precise set of tactics can guarantee success. What they can do is to help maximise the potential of the individual players.

Luis Figo in action. If midfield support is lacking, the strikers - or especially, a lone striker - can find themselves isolated or outnumbered.

Tactical decisions can give a team a vital edge, as the the margin between success and failure is often extremely small. A good system uses the individual strengths of the players to the full. If there are any obvious weaknesses in the team, a formation should be adopted which makes it difficult for the opposition to exploit them.

DEFENSIVE FORMATIONS

Defensively, the main considerations are how many players to use, and whether or not to deploy a sweeper. For many years, four defenders were considered the norm. These days, many attacking sides might play with just one or two strikers. Having spare defenders is all very well, but it means a team must be outnumbered elsewhere. This is one of the factors behind the introduction of wing-backs in a 3-5-2 system in recent years.

It was the defence-minded Italians of the 1960s who developed the idea of playing a sweeper or "*libero*" (free player) behind the marking defenders. His job is to cover across the whole back line, and he must also co-ordinate the offside trap. Although the use of a sweeper was originally conceived as an ultra-defensive tactic, teams gradually became aware of the attacking potential of the *libero*. In particular, the great Dutch and German sides of the 1970s recognised that the sweeper was in a prime position to break forward and launch attacks. Remember, a team should not simply decide it wants to operate a sweeper system; instead, the coach must look at his available players and decide whether anyone has the skills required for this highly specialised role.

MIDFIELD FORMATIONS

The midfield area is universally acknowledged as the most important battleground on the pitch. The team that controls the midfield controls the match. This fact has informed every coach's thinking concerning formations in the modern era. At one time, the 4-2-4 system was very common, with two playmakers linking the defence and attack. This gradually gave way to 4-3-3 and 4-4-2. Today, some teams operate a 4-5-1 system, particularly for away games. You can see from this pattern that there has been a tendency to pack the midfield by pulling strikers into deeper positions. The recent trend to play with wing-backs in a 3-5-2 formation has had a similar effect, but this time by pushing defenders forward.

Strength in midfield

Certainly no team can afford to be overrun in midfield. However, if four or even five players are operating in this area, it is vital that they drop deep to bolster the defence, and break forward to support the attack. Of course, midfielders shouldn't all go forward or fall back at the same time. Good players watch how the play is developing and cover for each other as required.

Midfield players like Malbranque (r) have a wide range of skills. Apart from their creative involvement they are strong defensively and are always an attacking threat.

Five forwards

Gone are the days when teams regularly lined up with five forwards. The 2-3-5 formation was very vulnerable defensively. ◀

Sweeper system

The great Dutch and German sides of the 1970s recognised that the sweeper was in a prime position to break forward and launch attacks. The Dutch philosophy of "total football" was based on the talents of Johan Cruyff. Ajax of Amsterdam won the European Cup with the 1-3-3-3 formation. ▶

ATTACKING FORMATIONS

4-4-2

Manchester United's success over the past decade has been founded on a basic 4-4-2 formation with midfield players quick to get forward to join the attack.

Robert Pires has the priceless quality of getting forward quickly to support the attacking play.

Gone are the days when teams regularly lined up with five forwards. Nowadays, the striker's role can be a very lonely one, particularly away from home. Most teams tend to play with two up front, sometimes only one. If other players join the attack, however, it can be devastating. Manchester United's success over the past decade has been founded on a basic 4-4-2 formation. The pace and fluid movement in the team have always meant that midfield players and defenders are quick to get forward when United are on the attack. If this kind of support is lacking, strikers - or the lone striker - can find themselves isolated and outnumbered.

Hunting in pairs

There is an old saying that strikers hunt in pairs. This can be a straightforward twin-pronged attack, or the more recent innovation of a split-striker set-up. In the latter system, one striker plays in a slightly withdrawn role. By dropping a little deeper, players in this position can sometimes find space more easily and make themselves difficult to mark. Teddy Sheringham and Paul Scholes are often used in this role to very good effect.

DEVELOPING TACTICS

There has been international club interest in the young US soccer sensation Freddy Adu, who played in the Under-17 World Cup Championship.

Young players shouldn't get too bogged down with theories about different formations and tactical ploys. Learning the individual skills and getting a feel for the ball is far more important at an early age. However, you are never too young to appreciate that football is a team game, and it isn't enough for eleven individuals to go out on to the pitch, no matter how talented they are.

For young players, skills come first. But as a player develops, an understanding of tactics becomes increasingly important.

Playing as a unit

A team that plays as a unit will always perform at a higher level than the individual talents of the players might suggest.

The skill of the coach is to look at his players and decide on a pattern of play that uses their talents to maximum advantage. That isn't enough, however. A pattern of play that works well on a certain day against particular opponents might prove ineffective the following week against a different team.

A team that plays as a unit will always perform at a higher level.

ATTACKING TACTICS

When considering the tactics most likely to yield goalscoring opportunities, perhaps it's no bad idea to think about what causes defenders most headaches. Defenders don't like being outnumbered, stretched across the pitch, dragged out of position or forced to turn and defend, facing their own goal. It follows that attackers should try to create these very situations as often as possible during a game. Let's look at each in turn.

Getting forward

Outnumbering defenders means getting players into forward positions. Very occasionally, you see a lone striker win the ball and score, even when he is surrounded by defenders. This is usually down to complacency, each defender leaving the marking duties to someone else. However, many more goals are scored when the attacking side can create a two-on-one or three-on-two situation. Midfield players can be particularly important in this regard. Late runs into the box can give a team a vital player advantage, and they are also very difficult for defences to cope with. Lee Bowyer is a player who excels at bursting forward to join the attack at exactly the right moment, and he regularly gets on the end of a move to knock the ball into the net.

Creating width

Stretching defences means playing with width. If the team doesn't have natural wingers, then other players should try to provide width. This could be one of the strikers, midfield players or full-backs.

To pull defenders out of position, attackers should keep on the move, twisting, turning, perhaps dropping deep, sometimes switching positions with team-mates.

Forcing defenders to turn can be achieved in many ways: a clever dribble, a deft flick-on, a flighted pass over the top, a low through-ball slotted between defenders.

James McFadden. The critical factor is getting the ball into the attacking third as often as possible and getting as many shots on target as possible.

Patient or direct?

Many teams like to play possession football as they probe for an opening. Others favour a more direct approach, getting the ball to the strikers as quickly as possible. The critical factor is getting the ball into the attacking third as often as possible and getting the maximum number of shots on target. The way a team gets the ball into the danger area will depend on the qualities of the players. If they are good at passing and moving, a slower build-up might reap rewards. On the other hand, if the moves are regularly breaking down after eight or ten passes and the team still hasn't got into the opposition's half, then these tactics aren't producing an end product. Similarly, if a team has defenders and midfielders who can spray long passes accurately, and front players who are good target men, then the long ball can certainly catch out defences.

Strike partnerships

"Strikers hunt in pairs." Look at any successful side and you will see how much truth there is in this old saying. Manchester United's Treble-winning side of 1999 was spearheaded by Dwight Yorke and Andy Cole, who were both in dazzling form all season.

The best strike partners seem to forge an almost telepathic understanding, each knowing instinctively what the other is going to do. They also tend to complement each other's skills.

In recent years, two factors have changed this traditional set-up somewhat, at the top level at least. One is the squad system. Many top sides now have four strikers on their books. This gives six possible strike pairings, and some will inevitably be more successful than others. Strikers need to play together regularly in order to gel, and the squad rotation system doesn't help in this regard.

Second, many teams now prefer to play one lone striker, with another in a deeper position. Teddy Sheringham is just about the best in the business in this withdrawn role. By dropping deep into the "hole" between the midfield and attack, he is able to find a lot of space. You need great vision and excellent delivery to play in this position, and Sheringham has both in abundance. He is superb at picking out his strike partner, or playing slide-rule passes into the path of midfield players and full-backs making forward runs.

Lone striker The 4-5-1 formation is used by many professional teams when playing away or against strong opposition. It is also employed in the counter-attack, when a team defends deep, soaks up pressure and breaks forward when possession is won. This is hard work for the central striker, who needs to have good abilities at holding up the ball until support arrives.

Support striker One striker plays in a slightly withdrawn role. By dropping a little deeper, players in this position can sometimes find space more easily and make themselves difficult to mark. Teddy Sheringham and Paul Scholes are often used in this role to very good effect.

Two wingers Playing with one central striker but with two wingers gives width but places a great responsibility on the midfield support. Ajax were very successful with this formation in the 1970s.

Arriving late

A late run into the penalty area can be hard to pick up.

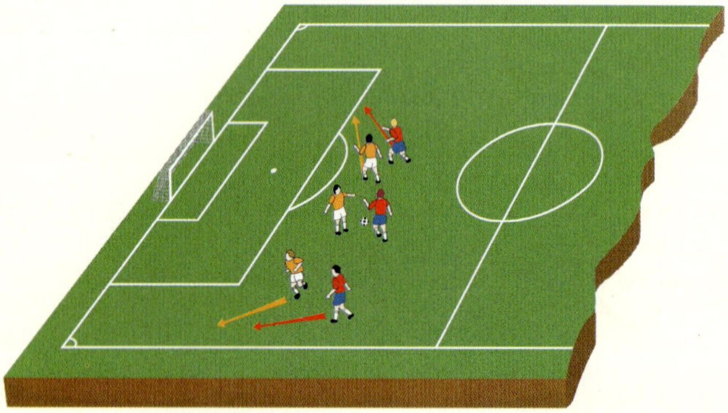

Creating space

Strikers can create space for the man on the ball by moving away and taking their markers with them.

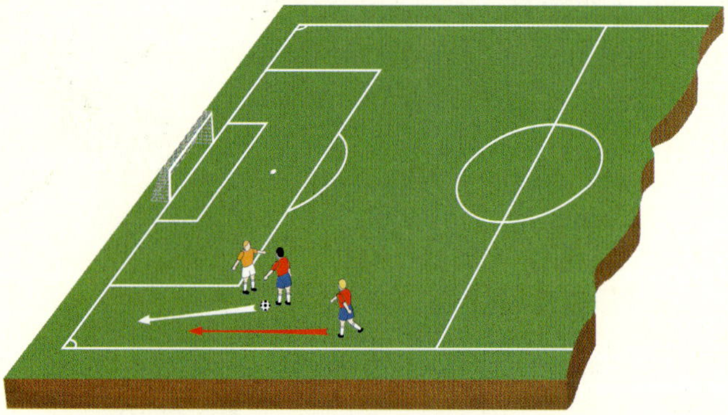

Overlapping full-backs

When defenders move up to support they can be very effective in getting near to the goal-line before delivering a cross.

The counter-attack

A feature of the modern game which contains elements of both attacking tactics already discussed is counter-attacking. It is a possession tactic, but it usually involves few players and few touches. It is also a direct tactic. Long passes and forward runs - both on and off the ball - also feature prominently. Defending deep, soaking up pressure and breaking forward when possession is won used to be regarded as a cautious approach, perhaps employed for away games. These days, counter-attacking is seen as a formidable attacking weapon. The reason is simple. If a team can turn defence into attack quickly, then the opposition won't have time to get themselves into ideal positions; they may struggle to get enough players behind the ball; they may get pulled out of position or turned round if the attacking side can get behind them. In other words, counter-attacking can create many of the situations that defenders fear most. Liverpool has enjoyed a lot of success with this method, and Manchester United has scored many goals just a few seconds and a few passes after the ball was in their goalkeeper's hands.

Overlapping full-back

Despite the current fashion for playing three centre-backs and wing-backs, the flat back four is still favoured by many top teams. Manchester United has enjoyed huge success using two full-backs alongside a twin pairing at the heart of the defence.

If the opportunity presents itself, full-backs should be just as ready to get forward as wing-backs. Players such as Gary Neville and Michael Silvestre are masters of attacking full-back play. They link up with the midfield players, help to create a numerical advantage over the opposing defence and also deliver quality crosses into the box. Even if they don't get the ball, they know they will be occupying a defender and making space for others to exploit.

Playing to strengths

Still on the theme of turning defence into attack, remember that winning the ball in the opposition's half creates a far more dangerous attacking platform than gaining possession near your own goal-line. Most teams tend to defend by retreating towards their own box and getting players behind the ball. This is a natural enough reaction, but in doing so, teams are sometimes missing a golden opportunity. If a midfielder or striker can win the ball, there will be far fewer opponents standing between him and the goal.

Finally, don't be tempted to look at Manchester United's or Arsenal's attacking style and try to emulate it in your team. It is only natural for youngsters to copy the individual skills and tricks of the top players, but when it comes to team tactics, a side should look at its own attacking strengths and exploit them to the full. In other words, develop your tactics around the players available, not the other way round.

Two up and one support

Often called playing "in the hole". The supporting player has more freedom and is harder to mark as he plays between the opposition's defenders and midfield players.

Kleberson of Manchester United in his goalscoring role can also cross well and give support to fellow strikers.

DEFENDING TACTICS

Defending is a combination of individual and collective strengths. Both are equally important. Good organisation and astute positional play can be let down by poor individual technique. Similarly, excellent individual defenders will struggle if they don't play as a unit. We have already looked at individual defending skills; let us now look at the tactical side of defending as a team.

Zonal defending

A defender covers a particular area of the pitch. If an attacker moves across the field, in an effort to create space, into a different zone - then another defender takes over the marking duties. In a system of five at the back, the full-backs have flexible roles.

Zonal marking or man-for-man

There are two broad defensive systems: zonal marking and man-for-man marking. In the first system, defenders cover a particular area of the pitch. If an attacker moves across the field in an effort to create space - into a different zone - then another defender takes over the marking duties. The advantage of this system is that defences tend to keep their shape, since the defenders are not pulled out of position. Problems can arise in the "grey" areas, where the zones overlap. Naturally, attackers will try to exploit any confusion in such areas.

In the man-for-man system, defenders mark individuals rather than space. When the opposition has the ball, defenders will mark a certain opponent and track him even if he switches positions. It is important that all players accept their share of defensive responsibilities in this system. For example, if a midfield player breaks forward, his opposite number must go with him, otherwise he may be leaving his defence a man short. Teams using a man-for-man marking system often employ a sweeper. He is a spare player who will provide cover for the markers and deal with any balls knocked into the space behind the defence.

Defending with numbers on the goal line. Charlton Athletic try in vain to keep out Southampton.

Getting goal-side

In practice, many teams use a combination of zonal marking and the man-for-man system. Whichever method is employed, it is important that all eleven players share the defensive responsibilities. Quite simply, if the opposition has the ball, then you are a defender. Even at the top level you can see forwards who only come to life when their team has the ball. This is poor play, for two reasons. First, an attacker who doesn't track back could be leaving his defence outnumbered. Second, it is much better - and more dangerous - if a team can win the ball back in advanced positions.

Even if defenders are not raiding forward, the attacking players shouldn't relax. They should harry and chase defenders when they are on the ball. The attacker might not win possession, but he might hurry the defender into making a poor pass. This is what is meant by "defending from the front".

Forcing an attacker inside

The covering defender goes towards the touch-line which pushes the attacker into the crowded midfield.

Marc Wilmots is closed down by defenders and shoots under pressure.

Delaying tactics

Ideally, defenders should only commit themselves to a tackle when they are sure of winning the ball. It doesn't always work out this way, of course. When a player is beaten, one of his team-mates must be ready to come and close the attacker down. The aim of the beaten defender should be to recover and get behind the ball as quickly as possible. To allow this to happen, his team-mate should jockey the attacker, forcing him towards the touchline or across the field.

Second line of defence

An attacker who successfully dribbles past a defender must be faced by another! Defenders must cover each other. If you have to leave the player you are marking to go and challenge for the ball, then it will be up to one of your team-mates to cover for you. No attacker should be able to get a clear sight of goal after beating only one opponent. Teams which do concede goals in this way are often guilty of being too square. That is when the deepest defenders are all in a line across the pitch. If an attacker can breach that line, either with a bit of individual trickery or by latching on to a through-pass, then he could have a goalscoring opportunity. Defences can counter this by defending with depth. This involves one defender dropping behind the others. He provides a second line of defence if a team-mate is beaten or if the ball is played into space. With some teams a different player will drop deep in different situations; others have a specialist for the job, the sweeper.

Defending in numbers

Football is a numbers game. If you regularly find yourself defending with a numerical disadvantage, your luck will run out sooner rather than later. In practice, this means getting players behind the ball once your team has lost possession. Defenders who are already in good positions should try to hold the attacking side at bay while their team-mates get goal-side. These delaying tactics are crucial, and include jockeying the attacker, pushing him infield or forcing him into a negative pass. Once a defender is goal-side, he should position himself so that both the player he is marking and the ball are in view at all times.

With players behind the ball, the team should apply pressure on the attacker in possession. That means cutting down his options. If the attacker can't get a shot in, and all possible forward passes are covered, then he might be forced into a negative pass or a dribble.

Ibrahim Ba of Bolton Wanderers tackles Lee Clark of Fulham. With Ibrahim Ba fully committed to the tackle, a team-mate goes to give cover.

The sweeper

The sweeper system was originally conceived by Italian coaches some 40 years ago. Italian defences were famous for their meanness, and employing a spare player to cover behind the markers made them even harder to score against. Later, Dutch and German teams began to exploit the attacking potential of the sweeper's role. He became a pivotal player, someone who could carry the ball out of defence and launch counter-attacks.

The single most important quality that a sweeper must have is the ability to read the game. He must spot any danger signs early on and adjust his position accordingly. He will also be the player who organises the offside trap.

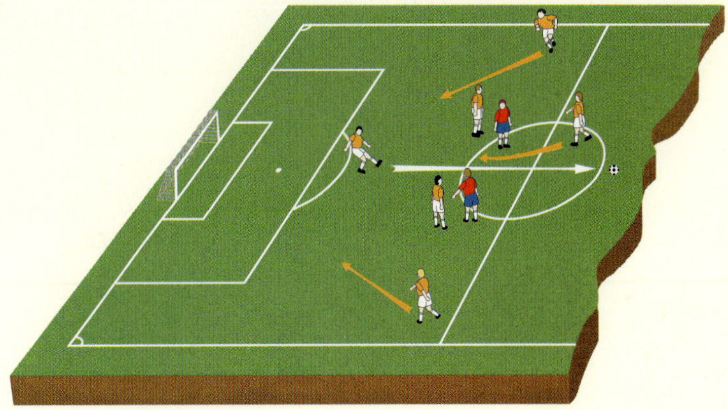

The sweeper

With some teams a different player will drop deep in different situations to act as cover; others have a specialist for the job, the sweeper.

Communication

One time when the defence certainly won't want to be in a ragged or staggered line is when playing the offside trap. The trap is a valuable defensive ploy, but only if all defenders are on the same wavelength. They should step up together as the ball is about to be played forward. Communication is vital. One player will often take responsibility for playing the offside trap, giving an agreed signal for the defence to move up. The attackers will either be stranded offside or forced to retreat themselves. But if one defender hangs back while the rest step forward, the whole strategy can unravel, with disastrous consequences.

Adrian Muti controls the ball. Defenders who are already in good position should try and hold the attacking side at bay while their team-mates get goal-side.

A compact defence is a tight defence. Even if a team is back in numbers, there will be many potentially dangerous gaps if the players are stretched right across the pitch. That's why full-backs should try to turn attacking wide players infield rather than down the touchline. They will be heading into a congested area where there will be very little time or space.

Finally, every goal will be down to a combination of good attacking play and poor defending. Pundits who are ex-professionals often betray their old playing position when they analyse goals. Former strikers such as Gary Lineker always like to applaud the attacker; former defenders such as Alan Hansen are always quick to highlight any defensive errors. In fact, very few goals are scored through sheer attacking brilliance. In the vast majority of cases - perfectionists might say all cases - every goal that is conceded is caused by some kind of defensive lapse.

Acknowledgements

Thanks to
Jane Hill, Richard Betts, Peter Wright,
Trevor Bunting, Simon Taylor,
Judy Spindler, Kelly Cantlon,
John Dunne, Oliver Clarke,
Daniel Groves, Jack Hylands,
Kilara Kilama-Oceng, Ubaid Nawaz,
Richard Trafford, Corinne Hill
Jen Little, Richard Whiting
and Natalie Jones.